DEMOCRATIC IDEALS AND THE VALUING OF KNOWLEDGE IN AMERICAN EDUCATION

Two Contradictory Tendencies

Henry R. Weinstock

and

Charles J. Fazzaro

Mellen Studies in Education
Volume 8

The Edwin Mellen Press
Lewiston/Queenston/Lampeter

Library of Congress Cataloging-in-Publication Data

Weinstock, Henry R.
   Democratic ideals and the valuing of knowledge in American
education : two contradictory tendencies / Henry R. Weinstock,
Charles J. Fazzaro.
      p.   cm. -- (Mellen studies in education ; v. 8)
   Includes bibliographical references.
   ISBN 0-88946-943-1
   1. Education--United States--Philosophy. 2. Education--United
States--Aims and objectives. 3. Knowledge, Theory of.
4. Democracy 5. Educational sociology--United States.
I. Fazzaro, Charles J. II. Title. III. Series.
LA217.W393 1990
370'.973--dc20
                                                       89-29794
                                                          CIP

This is volume 8 in the continuing series
Mellen Studies in Education
Volume 8 ISBN 0-88946-943-1
MSE Series ISBN 0-88946-935-0

A CIP catalog record for this book
is available from the British Library.

The Edwin Mellen Press
Box 450
Lewiston, New York
USA 14092

The Edwin Mellen Press
Box 67
Queenston, Ontario
CANADA L0S 1L0

The Edwin Mellen Press, Ltd.
Lampeter, Dyfed, Wales
UNITED KINGDOM SA48 7DY

Printed in the United States of America

To my wife, Joyce;
her children Juli, Vicki, and Keith;
and my children Kathy, Bess, and Timmy

HRW

To my parents

CJF

Contents

Introduction

This book constitutes an analysis and critique of the relationships between the means and ends of American public education. Central to the arguments presented herein is the assumption that the educational policies and practices of a society should be consistent with its sociopolitical philosophy. Given this assumption, American public education must have as its structural framework --its philosophy--the principles upon which the American liberal democratic social ideal rests. Essentially, these principles are reflections of values concerning the relationships that members of the American social order must seek to establish and maintain with each other and to their government.

Although abstract and often difficult to articulate, these values, nonetheless, are generally understood and deeply held. Evidence of this is overwhelming. America is unique in the annals of social democracies in that it is a society founded upon liberal democratic ideals, yet comprised of people with widely diverse social, ethnic, racial, and national/political backgrounds and cultures. In spite of this diversity, or perhaps because of it, each generation of Americans have governed themselves with a set of principles embodied in an uncharacteristically brief constitution that has remained essentially unchanged since its formulation and adoption 200 years ago.

Although the American social order is grounded in enduring and binding principles, the social contexts within which they find their expression are culturally dynamic and public; therefore, these abstract principles are in a constant state of being examined and redefined. Thus, on the one hand, these principles are *constituting*; and, on the other hand, their meanings are being continually *reconstituted*. This would be a logical contradiction if the principles were clearly definable and quantifiable, but they are not. They are, instead, expressions of values about human rights and relationships. Although enduring, these core values have eluded precise and universal understanding since the very beginning of organized societies.

Because the ideal American social order is grounded in abstract values, these values--and their concomitant political philosophy--need constant and unremitting clarification. Consequently, the United States could be viewed as an organized anarchy, at least to observers from societies that historically have been centrally controlled.[1] But the open, *qua* public, loosely connected, and multi-layered structure of our government is not simply an accident of history. As deliberately conceived by the Founding Fathers, the government was to be the people themselves, acting not solely in their own best individual interests but in the best interests of all others as well.

For those who are uncomfortable with sociopolitical structures that are not clearly defined, or for those who prefer a totalitarian structure, the system of government conceived in Philadelphia during that hot muggy summer of 1787 is not a comfortable alternative. The differences are clear. In totalitarian states, for example, all policies regulating the social order, including educational policies, are not publicly determined. Instead, they are conceived, promulgated, and enforced by powerful governmental elites. One need not search extensively in the history of civilizations to find a plethora of centrally controlled social systems, none of which endured for long without often resorting to brutal repression in order to dominate the masses. As the end of the twentieth century nears humankind is again witness to the disintegration of yet another repressive sociopolitical ideology, Soviet style communism.

But the mere existence of the Constitution, with its expression of liberal democratic principles, does not in itself guarantee that Americans will continue to govern themselves. It was clear to at least some of the Founding Fathers, such as Thomas Jefferson, that essential to bringing these democratic and individualistic aims to full fruition was an educated citizenry, educated "at the common expense of all."[2] Jefferson clearly understood the significant role that public education should, in fact, must play in not only preserving American democratic ideals but in providing all individuals with opportunities to acquire the knowledge and skills to be able to be fully empowered with their "unalienable Rights."[3] For this political philosophy to maintain and be fulfilled, the American system of education clearly must be structured so as to thoroughly promote throughout the broader society what Aristotle defined as "practical wisdom"--the wisdom or knowledge that promotes a person to act politically in a moral, just, and virtuous manner.

What we argue herein is that the Jeffersonian ideal of the relationship of education to democracy has been slowly and substantively subverted. More specifically, we conclude that the system of American public education is almost imperceptibly becoming an instrument of domination. This conclusion is supported by the contradictions which exist between the fundamental policies and practices (means) of American public education and the most widely accepted principles of the American liberal democratic ideal (ends).

This work was undertaken on the premise that if there are contradictions between the means and ends of American public education, then they logically could be revealed through an analysis and concomitant critique of both historical and current educational policies and practices.

Conceptual Framework

To carry out this analysis and critique, a variety of analytical frameworks were used. One is a model *for* theorizing,[4] a model that deals with the epistemological implications associated with the valuing of knowledge. In order to simplify the discussions, and yet not lose the essence of the analytical dimensions of this work, the model sharply dichotomizes the valuing of knowledge as being either *intrinsic* (for its own sake) or *instrumental* (for its need and/or use). For determining the legitimacy of educational policies and practices, the model is nested within the framework of the fundamental principles of the American democratic ideal. This analytical scheme is used in conjunction with the logical and linguistic analysis of the language of education.[5]

Lastly, in order to strengthen the analysis, the legitimacy of educational policies and practices was continually filtered through the framework of a means-ends critique. Taken together, these approaches are a reflection of the authors' respective academic backgrounds and current interests in the search for more powerful conceptual tools to examine American public education.

Intended Outcomes

Because both the analysis and critique are at the broadest levels of the relationships between public education and the social order, the outcomes of this work are intended to serve largely as heuristic schemes for generating further analyses and critiques. In light of this intended purpose, the reader must keep in mind that the analytical tools employed in this effort are essentially conceptualizing models, that is, models *for* theory rather than models *of* theory. Models *of* theory have both preconceived means and ends. The various philosophical *isms* would be examples of models *of* theories. On the other hand, models *for* theory are characteristic models. That is, they have no preconceived means and/or ends. Thus, these models have the potential to give rise to a multitude of theories, each of which, in turn, might serve as structures for recommended practices.

Because models *for* theorizing are used in this analysis, then, unlike the requirements of models *of* theories, thorough discussions of the numerous arguments that surround wide ranges of policies and practices in American education are beyond the scope of this book. We clearly recognize and agree that philosophical analyses should be undertaken for critically examining and subsequently explicating the more functional aspects of American public education. But in order for such a task to be fruitful, an essential prerequisite must be an analysis and critique of the relationship of broad educational policies and practices to American democratic ideals. It is precisely with the latter requirement in mind that we undertook this project.

Contextual Considerations

Unlike what is reflected in many of the current educational policies and practices, this work recognizes the fact that all educational activities, being distinctly human, take place within particular social realities which are constituted by the members of unique social groups. Both the analytical and critical dimensions of this work are consistent with the current assumption that the academic structures of public schools are primarily and fundamentally influenced by the expectations of the social environments in which each school exists. Because the instrumental valuing of knowledge has been widespread and deeply ingrained in the broader culture, at least in Western societies over the past two centuries, then it is reasonable to conclude that the valuing of knowledge in the public schools has become essentially instrumental as well. We believe that the discussions herein will give readers a framework for understanding how the growing influence of the instrumental valuing of knowledge upon the academic structures of public schools has led to contradictions between the policies and practices (means) of schooling and the fundamental principles of the American sociopoiltical order (ends).

Literary Considerations

In committing this analysis and critique to writing, the prospective readership of both the broad spectrum of academic and lay persons interested in educational issues was a primary consideration--particularly in the presentation of the more theoretical and philosophical arguments. So as not to detract from the heuristic and generative intent of the arguments, and in order to maintain both theoretical and temporal continuity, we have organized this book into only five relatively short chapters, each beginning with a comprehensive overview. Likewise, references and notes have been kept to a minimum.

NOTES

1. See, for example, Alexis De Tocqueville, *Democracy in America*. Volume II. ed. P. Bradley (New York: Vintage Books, 1954).

2. See Thomas Jefferson, *Preamble to a Bill for the More General Diffusion of Knowledge*. Paul Liecester Ford (ed.). *The Works of Thomas Jefferson* (1779). Vol. II, Federal Edition (New York: G. P. Putnam's Sons, 1904), pp. 414-26.

3. For a discussion of the ideal relationship of public education to the Constitution, see Charles J. Fazzaro, "The U.S. Constitution as a Philosophy of Education: Implications for Rationality and Legitimacy." *Proceedings of the Southwestern Philosophy of Education Society* 37 (1987): 97-104.

4. For a more complete discussion of models and their uses, see Henry R. Weinstock, "The Concept of Model and Educational Research," *Journal of Research in Science Teaching* 4, no.1 (1966): 45-51.

5. For a more complete discussion of the use of linguistic analysis, see Henry R. Weinstock, "On Philosophical Problems Subject to Ordinary Language Analysis," *Journal of Thought* 6, no. 1 (January 1971): 38-48.

One

Education and the Valuing of Knowledge

Overview

The position taken in this analysis and critique is that *idealism* and *realism* historically have been the two major philosophical perspectives in the Western world, both having their origins in the intellectually fertile Classical period of early Greece. Plato (427-347 B.C.) is credited with first advancing idealism as a worldview. He believed that it was through "ideas" created within the mind that each person was able to constitute their own particular view of the world, *qua* reality. Subsequently, because of the uniqueness of each individual, Plato's "idealism" implies that there is the potential, at least, for the existence of an unlimited number of competing explanations of the world, or "rationalities." On the other hand, Aristotle (384-322 B.C.), a student of Plato, believed that the "real" world exists independent of the mind. Unlike idealism, Aristotle's "realism" implies only a single rationality, one to be discovered by the mind rather than one being uniquely constituted by it. Thus, it logically can be concluded that because ideas--mere theories or structures of reality--are central to idealism, then idealists primarily value knowledge *intrinsically*--for its own sake. On the other hand, because realists believe that it is only through knowledge that one can perceive the "real" world, then it can logically be concluded that realists primarily value knowledge *instrumentally*--for its usefulness. These two fundamental worldviews, idealism and realism, and their respective value orientations, essentially dominated Western intellectual thought up to the reign of the Roman emperor Constantine the Great (288?-337 A.D.). It was Constantine who, through the Edict of Milan (313 A.D.), made Christianity a lawful religion throughout the entire Roman empire, an act of great significance.

Soon after the reign of Constantine, Christianity became the dominant force in virtually all aspects of life in the Western world. In particular, its influence on knowledge became absolute. The official early Christian view was that all "true" knowledge was revealed by God; thus, seeking the "truth" other than through God was not only an inane pursuit but heretical as well. This widespread belief in revealed "truth" not only effectively stopped the search for new "earthly" knowledge to explain the world, but also the pursuit of knowledge simply for its own sake. Fortunately, a great deal of the "earthly" knowledge that existed at this stage of Western history was preserved in many Christian monasteries.

It was through the efforts of the great theologian-scholar Saint Augustine (354-430 A.D.) that these monasteries were popularized as centers of Christian learning.[1] Grounded in a blend of theology and Neo-Platonic idealism, as exemplified in Augustine's *The City of God*, new knowledge, what there was of it, essentially was valued intrinsically. Thus, from the time of Constantine the Great to about 1200 A.D., the only acceptable "truth" was that officially sanctioned by the Church, which became the unifying institution of Western society. But regardless of this official orthodoxy, it was within the *librariums* in the monasteries, especially those adhering to the Rule of Saint Benedict, that brave scholars kept the light of knowledge burning during the Dark Ages by preserving and protecting already existing knowledge.

After 1200 A.D. the writings of many Greek scholars, particularly those of Aristotle, as well as Arab mathematics, science, and logic, slowly became available to the scholars within the developing universities in Europe. This brought about a shift from an almost pseudo-idealism to Aristotelian realism as the basic worldview which was to shape the emerging modern Western society. This shift was particularly apparent in the works of Church scholars such as Thomas Aquinas (1225-1274) and his *Summa Theologica*.[2] The shift was so pronounced that soon after the canonization of Aquinas in 1323 A.D., *Summa Theologica* became the foundation of the new theology of the Church.

After the thirteenth century and until the time of the Enlightenment, the credibility of knowledge was dependent upon its consistency with the new theology. Grounded in an Aristotelian philosophical view of nature, the new theology justified "truth" through logic and observations. Still, this method of justification was significantly different from the modern-day scientific method, which depends not only on observation but also on the validation of conclusions through experimentation. Among the early efforts in this direction was that of Roger Bacon (1214-1292 A.D.), who first proposed the scientific method to Pope Clement IV. But Clement died in 1268 A.D., leaving Bacon alone to face his doubters. Trapped in the ideology of the Dark Ages, Bacon's opponents quickly saw to it that he was imprisoned, where he remained until his death in 1292 A.D., about 400 years before the broad acceptance of the scientific method.[3]

Although the medieval view of the world was grounded in Platonic idealism, its reliance on philosophy kept alive not only idealism but realism as well. This was particularly evident through the spirit of inquiry that existed in at least some medieval monasteries. Through their teaching, those monastic scholars with inquiring minds thus became models for the first scholars that began to gather in small "communities"--the first universities--to teach, exchange ideas, and to study. Universities were first recognized as "communities" or "corporations" of scholars as early as the beginning of the thirteenth century. These early universities were even given notice by the Church. In fact, in 1205 A.D., Pope Innocent, in addressing the masters and students at the now University of Paris, wrote "*Universis magistris et scholarebus Parisiensibus*" or (loosely translated) "to the masters and scholars of the University of Paris."[4] Although most of the scholars of the medieval universities were less interested in interpreting the *corpus academicum* of set books than in the passing on of a crystallized culture, some did pursue knowledge for spiritual and intellectual health.[5] But others, with more inquiring minds, were interested in pursuing knowledge for its own sake. It was from this primeval intellectual mass of scholars that the university ideal evolved.

Idealism and realism were eventually represented in the early universities respectively in the liberal arts (joined later by the sciences) and in the professional schools. These competing values of knowledge are at the center of the dynamic political nature of university governance and society's view of the university.[6] The structural and political dynamics of the university thus become important factors in modern societies that use the university as a primary institution for the preparation of teachers for their public schools. It is for this reason that an analysis of the relationship between democratic ideals and the valuing of knowledge must begin with the university and its influence on the valuing of knowledge within the broader society in general and public education in particular. That knowledge can be valued *intrinsically*, that is for its own sake, or *instrumentally*, by its perceived utility. It is a dichotomy uniquely suited for framing this analysis.

The competition between the intrinsic and instrumental valuing of knowledge has intensively manifested itself both in the university, through the advent of the "new" professional schools, and in the public schools, through the modern educational ideology of Progressive Education. Within modern universities the conflicts in the valuing of knowledge are exacerbated by both a natural rivalry between colleges of arts and sciences and professional schools and among the professional schools themselves. A major factor in precipitating these conflicts in the valuing of knowledge evolved because schools of education within universities had to increasingly assume responsibility for the task of preparing teachers for the many new public high schools that were being established by the turn of the twentieth century. Internally, these schools of education were also not without conflict. In particular, ideological disputes were frequent and divisive between professors of elementary education and professors of secondary education.

Presently, there are many fundamental contradictions that generally exist between the structure and functions of higher education and teacher education. These contradictions are the result of a variety of factors including (1) early criticisms of the public high school movement, (2) societal pressures to have public institutions of higher education take a major role in the preparation of teachers to teach not only in the new high schools but elementary schools as well, and (3) the role that university faculties in the arts and sciences were to play in teacher education. The latter became a particularly volatile issue as the fundamental value of knowledge in the broader society shifted from the intrinsic to one predominantly instrumental. In higher education this shift manifested itself politically in the fact that, by mere legislative fiat, many state normal schools and teachers colleges were transformed almost overnight into state colleges and later into "universities."

1. Valuing Knowledge in the University

Knowledge can be valued intrinsically, that is for its own sake, or instrumentally, by need and/or use.[7] This division of knowledge became notable in the American public schools during the 1930s. It was clearly evident in the sharp contrast between the essentialism that was dominant in the academic structures of the high schools and the modern educational ideology of Progressive Education that was evolving in the elementary schools. The value of these approaches to education spawned widespread and lengthy debates not only among educators but the general public as well. Chief among the protagonist in this valuing of knowledge conflict were those at the university, where the traditional intrinsic valuing of knowledge was still dominant.

Within the university itself the conflict between the intrinsic versus the instrumental valuing of knowledge also became intense, particularly with the advent of the "new" professional schools.[8] The basic assumptions and justifications giving rise to the establishment of these new professional schools was to many a total contradiction to the philosophy that the university exemplified. This philosophy was grounded in the tradition that developed in Western universities during the Renaissance. It was during this time that knowledge was often pursued without any regard for its practicality, its "usefulness."

A consequence of this conflict in the valuing of knowledge was the charge by the university traditionalists that those in the new professional schools were simply pure instrumentalists. This belief was supported by the fact that professional schools would simply "pick and choose" from available knowledge only that which they believed was useful. But the traditionalists claimed that this "useful" knowledge was largely gleaned from the knowledge generated through the intrinsic pursuit of the "truth" by professors in the liberal arts and sciences within the university. Subsequently, these early conflicts between the arts and sciences and the professional schools were likely the rootcause of major problems with internal governance, day-to-day operations, and faculty morale that exist in many universities today. This controversy surrounding the intrinsic/instrumental valuing of knowledge conflict within universities not only has implications for the legitimacy of higher education in America, but also for its public schools and democratic social structures as well.

Instrumentalism and Today's University

In higher education today there is clearly a significant increase in the number of professional school graduates in comparison to arts and sciences graduates.[9] Since the professional schools in many universities are attracting an ever-growing majority of students, the fundamental value of knowledge at these universities is more likely to be instrumental rather than intrinsic. The result of this shift has transformed the university degree from a credential signifying "knowing" to a credential signifying "being able to do." Because ways of "doing" are often subject to change, this raises questions about the legitimacy of the claim that a degree from a present-day university has permanent and lasting educational value.

Professional schools are primarily concerned with the kind of knowledge that the professional school faculties consider important for practical applications. If not exclusively, at least a very large portion of this knowledge clearly is taken from the basic research of the arts and sciences. Applications of this knowledge can be found in the curriculums and programs of such professional schools as business, engineering, communications, and social work. Because of the temporal nature of most practical applications, the basic knowledge that is turned into practical knowledge often is also accorded a temporal status as well. Unlike the enduring curriculums of the arts and sciences, the constant selectivity of the knowledge that constitutes the base of professional schools results in ever-changing programs and courses, thus making the curriculums of professional schools temporal. Yet it is equally true that the legitimacy and status of the university in American society depends on how the university reacts to threats to its academic foundation.

The academic foundation of Western universities was developed over many centuries and is based upon knowledge which has permanence and endurance. Western universities have been able to maintain this position because the broader society has respected the concept of academic freedom. Until recently, at least, this has allowed universities to remain somewhat immune from direct external political pressures to change their views of knowledge in order to conform to the values of the larger society. But subtle and indirect pressures from society are causing significant changes in university academic structures and, subsequently, the way universities fundamentally value knowledge. The nature of these changes is evident in the academic structures of the professional schools.

The ever-changing curriculums of the professional schools are a reflection of pressures from the economic "marketplace." These pressures parallel pressures that affect private industry and business. Likewise, it is the marketplace that essentially establishes the knowledge requirements for the hiring of faculty members of professional schools. Universities are under considerable pressure to pay marketplace salaries in order to attract and retain faculty members for their professional schools. On the other hand, the traditional university faculty positions, such as those in history, English, foreign languages, and the arts, have few if any marketplace correlates. The knowledge requirements for becoming a member of these faculties is determined purely by those within the university. And, since the university liberal arts and (to a lesser degree) sciences have little if any competition in the broad economic marketplace, their salaries are usually much lower on average than those in professional schools.[10] As a consequence, serious distortions in not only salaries, but also in physical facilities and related services, have generated marked differences between the professional schools and the arts and sciences.[11] In today's universities these distortions have led to a competition of interests between pursuing knowledge intrinsically--for its own sake--or pursuing knowledge instrumentally--for its "marketplace" value.

As it was noted earlier, the pronounced and persistent emphasis on materialism in the broader society, via the instrumental valuing of knowledge, has serious implications for the university. The most important of these is society's misconception of how important the open-ended and unrestricted pursuit of knowledge is for the American democracy. Historically, it has been the university which has championed such a liberal approach to knowledge, which essentially is the intrinsic valuing of knowledge embodied in the university ideal. But due to society's lack of an adequate understanding of the fundamental nature of the university, continued pressure is being brought to bear on the university to "produce" more "practical" knowledge.[12] Since the instrumental valuing of knowledge is becoming increasingly more dominant in the university, an analysis of the historical development of the American university might shed some light on the consequences of this shift in knowledge valuing.

The Academic Structure of American Universities

American universities evolved through the efforts of such nineteenth-century educators as Henry Philip Tappan who, after visiting European universities in the early 1850s, particularly those in Germany, made recommendations which set the pattern for the modern American university.[13] During the 1870s several of the larger American universities showed obvious signs of German influence. These universities included Cornell, Johns Hopkins, and Vanderbilt.[14] Their structures were based on the traditional model of a college of arts and sciences surrounded by a graduate school and the traditional professional schools of medicine, law, and theology. This structure was first adopted in America at Johns Hopkins. Its first president, Daniel Coit Gilman, was inaugurated in 1876. Gilman was responsible for structuring Johns Hopkins as primarily a graduate school having a "Faculty of Philosophy" as its central core.[15] It was much later that the central core became the arts and sciences.[16] Like those of the European universities, the distinguishing characteristics of the professoriate in these early American universities was a focus on fundamental knowledge without justification for its need and/or use.

Within the environment of the central core an even greater intrinsic pursuit of knowledge took place in the specializations within the arts and sciences, this occurring at the graduate level. Only students of proven academic achievement were admitted to these graduate level programs, and only the best students of this select group emerged with a master's degree. Unlike the baccalaureate degree, the program of study and the time for completion of the masters degree was not well defined. The ultimate stage of graduate work in these American universities eventually became the Doctor of Philosophy degree, a level which few reached. The program of study for the doctorate was even less clearly defined than was that for the master's degree. Thus, the traditional passing of the "cloak of knowledge" from one generation of the professoriate to the next in any given field of study was an arduous and tenuous process indeed. The intrinsic pursuit of knowledge, and the resulting place of such knowledge in the arts and sciences curriculum was generally neither orderly, cooperative, nor emotionally reinforcing. Because of its intrinsic nature, the scholarly path of the doctoral candidate was constantly in the process of evolving.

Other influences in the scholarly path of the candidate were more political in nature. These political influences generally emanated from the competition between different schools of thought. Even within narrow academic disciplines professors competed with one another to have their particular view of knowledge prevail within those disciplines. These battles over the legitimacy of knowledge were further aggravated by the limited resources available to most universities. Thus, a political struggle began to take place between the arts and sciences and the professional schools. This manifested itself in the arts and sciences faculties often being described as living in an "ivory tower," whereas professional school faculties were considered to be in the "real world," since they laid claim to knowledge that was primarily "practical" and useful.[17]

The New Professional Schools

Although the distinctly scholarly pursuits of medicine, law, and theology were present in the early days of the American university, interest in the application of knowledge derived from the study of these disciplines was also evident. Medical schools, in order to create their own academic programs, looked for "useful" knowledge in such fields as biology, chemistry, physics, and mathematics. Often, attempts to make knowledge instrumental had the effect of devaluing the purely intrinsic pursuit of knowledge through inquiry that was present in the traditional arts and sciences. For example, if a professor's inquiry into an area of knowledge did not soon show practical implications for the training of future physicians, then any continued efforts by that professor were in various ways discouraged by the institution. Even medical school professors who were primarily interested in the practice of medicine often accused those professors who were primarily interested in the study (i.e., theoretical aspects) of medicine of being impractical and dealing with things that were irrelevant to the public's present health needs. This attitude about the immediate practicality of knowledge tended to limit the academic freedom of the faculties of medical schools. Because of the growing status of medical schools, this limiting of academic freedom effected other academic units of the university as well.

Pressures from the larger social environment for the immediate application of knowledge became the driving force behind just how the faculties of the new professional schools were to conduct their academic affairs. It thus became increasingly apparent to universities that in order to maintain their legitimacy in an increasingly consumer-oriented society they had to accommodate both the needs of the professional schools and their preference for practical knowledge. Likewise, arts and sciences faculties began to increasingly realize that in order to maintain their central position in the university they would eventually have to become partners, albeit often unwilling, in the production of knowledge that had a potential, at least, for having applied value.

One example of the arts and sciences being affected by the need for "practical" knowledge was in the field of electrical engineering which was emerging during the latter quarter of the nineteenth century. At that time the physics departments in universities were the repositories for knowledge about electricity. Yet the needs of the infant field of electrical engineering began to make increasingly greater demands on physics departments for more applied courses. As a consequence of both the reluctance of physics professors being forced into applied fields of study and the insistence of external influences, universities rapidly began to develop electrical engineering as an applied field of study separate from that of physics.[18] Similar processes were also taking place in other areas of engineering and in other fields dependent upon applied knowledge.

By the beginning of the twentieth century many new professional schools were already part of the American university scene. Included among these were schools of business administration[19] and journalism, among others.[20] The institutionalizing of these new professional schools within the university structure significantly limited the intrinsic pursuit of knowledge by many in the professoriate.

The "Professionalizing" of Knowledge

As discussed above, external societal influences increasingly began to control the basic academic structures of universities to a much greater degree than in the past. One of the major factors in this control was the growing number of fields of endeavor in the broader society that were struggling to gain recognition as "professions." Universities responded to this pressure by actively promoting these emerging fields of "professional" knowledge within their structures. This meant that new professional schools would more likely hire new faculty members whose prior academic preparation and experience would support a particular line of inquiry consistent with the "practical" knowledge needs of the school. As a consequence, only practical aspects of knowledge began to dominate their curriculums. This domination was largely insured by limiting the granting of tenure to only those professional school professors who did not seriously deviate from an interest in the pure application of knowledge.

The professional schools insured the domination of practical knowledge in their curriculums through other means as well. For instance, they increased the ratio of part-time adjunct to full-time faculty members. In schools of business these adjuncts were hired from business and industry to teach various "practical" aspects of their areas of expertise. Also, business, industrial, and philanthropic interests often contributed scholarships, endowments, and even academic chairs predicated on the pursuit of their respective applied fields. The new professional schools enhanced their presence on university campuses even further by aggressively recruiting students for their specialized applied fields.

In addition, the creation of junior/community colleges, which began as an extension of the high school but soon developed into a cross between the high school and the university, further bifurcated the intrinsic/instrumental dichotomy created through the increasing professionalization of knowledge.[21] The new junior/community colleges, for instance, granted college credit for courses taught by faculty members who were often actually craftsmen or employees from local industries. Soon these same institutions began to exert pressure on universities to accept transfer credit for what at least appeared to be academically comparable courses. As a consequence, the educational preparation for teaching courses in the arts and sciences programs increasingly came into conflict with the educational preparation for teaching courses in professional schools.

Other Challenges to the Intrinsic Valuing of Knowledge

The intrinsic pursuit of knowledge by university professors also became less valued due to the shifting values in the broader society from a future-time orientation to a present-time orientation. For example, the value of "a penny saved is a penny earned" was rejected in favor of "buy now pay later." This fundamental shift in values precipitated the view that professors in professional schools should not mirror their colleagues in the arts and sciences who value knowledge intrinsically. Rather, the professional school professors were expected to value only that knowledge which had practical worth; they were to value knowledge instrumentally. This, in turn, would help legitimate their professional fields of study in the wider society.

No longer were only physicians, lawyers, and ministers to be cloaked with the aura of the university. The new professionals, including accountants, journalists, and a plethora of others, began to share with the older professions the legitimacy gained from the rational myths that exist within the broad society about the university ideal. As a consequence, professional schools increasingly began to select from the arts and sciences only that knowledge which they needed to apply to their specific professional fields. This selection of knowledge also became true for certain schools outside of colleges of arts and sciences. Although some considered these schools to be "professional," others, for various reasons, did not accord them this status. The major example were schools of education, academic entities becoming increasingly prominent on the university scene at that time.

The importance of schools of education within traditional universities was that they provided a direct link between the universities and the public schools. Because of the environmental press resulting from beliefs about the nature and functions of public education, state governments soon began to indirectly influence the structure of the university. The major thrust of this influence was requiring public school teachers to meet certain educational requirements and standards in order to qualify for a teaching license. Thus, the links between public education and the university became stronger while the links between the university and its past became increasingly attenuated. Because of the relationship between the university and public education and the implications that this relationship has for valuing knowledge, the analysis herein demands a thorough consideration of this relationship.

2. The University Ideal and Public Education

Within university academic communities, schools of education are generally referred to as professional schools. Yet there are critics who maintain that describing schools of education as "professional" schools is inaccurate. When these critics are members of university faculties, there are at least two explanations for their views. The first stems from the natural rivalry among the professional schools--the nature of which is too complex to be discussed here. The second explanation centers on the intrinsic versus instrumental valuing of knowledge controversy that exists between professional schools and the arts and sciences. Because schools of education are the institutional links between universities and public education, it is a clarification of this conflict in the valuing of knowledge that best explains this linkage and the role of schools of education within university structures.

Schools of Education Within Universities

Within universities, schools of education are like colleges of arts and sciences in at least one fundamental way.[22] Schools of education are partners with the arts and sciences in perpetuating the intrinsic valuing of knowledge within the broader society. This is so even though professors in schools of education, unlike their colleagues in the arts and sciences, do not exclusively value knowledge intrinsically. A useful model to help explain this connection and shared role between a school of education and the arts and sciences in a university was developed by Kingsley Price at Johns Hopkins University in the 1950s.[23] Price advanced the argument that the role of the discipline of education in the university is the deliberate study of *how* knowledge developed in the arts and sciences is transmitted. In this regard the faculty of a school of education is logically not involved in producing new kinds of fundamental knowledge traditionally associated with the arts and sciences. Rather, the education faculty should, in every way possible, understand both the nature of fundamental knowledge *and* how it is transmitted to the masses.

For the arguments presented here it is important to remember that each member of the arts and sciences faculty has gained access to that faculty by demonstrating mastery of a particular fundamental field of knowledge-- an academic discipline. But university arts and sciences faculties are not in a position to transmit to the masses of a truly democratic society the knowledge and ways of knowing necessary for such a society to completely fulfill and maintain its democratic ideals. The reasons for this are manifold. Some of the more obvious are: (1) the sheer inability to reach all people in society that might be capable of gaining such knowledge; (2) the differences of opinion among the faculty of the arts and sciences on just what knowledge should be transmitted to the society as a whole; (3) local and regional disagreements within the broad society on exactly what knowledge all ought to learn; (4) local and regional political pressures for particular social and economic aims to be fostered by the public schools; and (5) the diminished value within the American society for the pursuit of most things perceived to be esoteric and abstract, especially activities such as pursuing knowledge for its own sake.

In the American society, at least, the general lack of valuing knowledge for its own sake stems from the gradual decline of idealism as a legitimate worldview in Western society. Although this decline began at least as early as the institutionalizing of Christianity in the Western world, it accelerated rapidly in the 1600s. This is particularly well illustrated by John Locke's criticisms of idealism in his famous *Essay Concerning Human Understanding*, published in 1690. If idealism indeed is the foundation of the intrinsic pursuit of knowledge, then teachers in the public schools are logically confronted with a dilemma. The nature of this dilemma can be better understood in light of the evolution of the field of education within the academic structure of higher education.

The Evolution of Education as an Academic Field

In early America, teachers were expected to teach the basic elements of an education, namely reading, writing, and arithmetic.[24] At that time these basic elements essentially constituted the whole of America's interest in educating the masses. Eventually, state-supported "normal schools" were developed to prepare teachers for the expanding system of common schools.[25] Much later, the modern school of education evolved within the American university as a response to broad societal demands to go beyond the teaching of the basic elements of reading, writing, and arithmetic. Also, many European immigrants wanted their children to achieve a level of education considerably beyond that of simple literacy. Thus there developed pressure both within and outside of public education to incorporate more of the knowledge of the arts and sciences within a general education designed for *all* students.

The meteoric expansion of public secondary education in America is clear evidence that society wanted significantly more of the kind of education that a high school diploma represented. When immigrants began arriving in sufficiently large numbers in the late 1800s they found mainly private tuition academies, which they could not easily afford, and comparatively few free public high schools. But by 1910, the number of free public high schools had increased nearly fivefold, from approximately 2,500 to over 10,000.[26] On the other hand, by 1900 the number of private tuition academies had drastically decreased compared to those that existed in 1850.[27]

It can be logically assumed that the educational aspirations of the immigrants were to a large degree materialistically motivated in that many of the immigrants wanted their children to be more economically prosperous than, for example, common laborers, store clerks, tailors, or shoemakers. But there were other factors that motivated the immigrants to doggedly pursue educational opportunities. Included among these was the desire that their children should attain a higher social/cultural status. Thus the immigrants viewed the public high schools as a means for their children to not only attain economic security but, through the study of history, music, art, drama, and languages, to also attain a higher cultural status as well.

The Evolution of the American High School Teacher

Teachers that taught in the private tuition academies of the 1800s predominantly had classical education backgrounds. Their expertise in the classics, ancient Roman and Greek history, geometry, classical drama, and the like, clearly reflected the educational and social values of the culture of that segment of American society which could afford to send their children to these academies. But, because there were relatively few of these classically prepared teachers, there was an inadequate supply of qualified teachers to staff the large number of high schools that were rapidly developing in the later 1800s.

And, there was little likelihood that there ever would be sufficient numbers of classically educated teachers to staff these new schools. Even if there was a sufficient number of these teachers it is likely that they would not have been fully accepted by the students and their parents. After all, most prospective high school students at that time were from a social/cultural strata drastically different from that of the teachers who were then teaching in the academies. These and related issues thus presented a major dilemma for those responsible for developing and staffing the new high schools. But the pressure for changes in the type of teachers that were to staff the new high schools came from various critics of the academic structure of public education. The concerns of many of these critics were based on broader social issues that they perceived to be educational as well. Thus, many of their concerns were only indirectly related to teacher preparation.

Compounding the problems presented by a difference in culture and social class between the public high school students and the teachers in the academies was an evolving disillusionment that many immigrants had with the American economic system. Due to the prevailing capitalistic philosophy of the relationship of business to labor, as well as political factors and general discrimination and mistrust of foreigners, many immigrant families found that they were not able to achieve their desired material gains. Some believed that their old world names, dress, habits, lack of marketable skills, and general cultural backwardness were responsible for their lack of success in the American society. Thus, in order for their children to more easily acquire good jobs after completing high school, many immigrants changed their names, dress, and language. This paralleled many hard-fought political struggles to bring about both greater access to educational opportunities and more equitable distribution of educational resources. Directly and indirectly, all of these factors and many others helped to bring about substantive changes in the basic academic structure of the American public high school. The demands for change which had begun with a whisper had now grown to a roar.

The subsequent changes in the academic structures of the new public high schools, as compared to the traditional private academies, were clearly reflected in fundamental changes in the traditional classical curriculum of the early public high schools. The changing academic structure increasingly began to exhibit applicable, practical, useful, and even vocational characteristics. By the 1930s teachers colleges began to gain significant popularity as legitimate institutions to prepare teachers for not only grammar schools but for the new public high schools as well.[28] This was in contrast to the many normal schools then in existence whose exclusive function was to prepare grammar school teachers. As a result, the education of the prospective public high school teachers in these new teachers colleges was oriented increasingly toward serving both the practical side of a child's future, in terms of instrumental economic needs, and the aesthetic side, in terms of intrinsic cultural needs. Thus, the academic preparation model which had evolved for the public high school teacher was significantly different from that which had typified the preparation of teachers for the private tuition academies.

The Core Curriculum

One major consequence of the shift from the purely classical or cultural tradition of the private academies to the practical *and* cultural curriculum of the public high schools was the "core curriculum." The core curriculum evolved during the 1930s as a consequence of the efforts of progressive educators and philosophers such as John Dewey. The core curriculum was a significant departure from the classical curriculum in that it did not emphasize traditional intrinsically valued subject matter. In the core curriculum the traditional academic areas of history, political science, and economics were simply grouped together as "social studies." Similarly, English, modern foreign languages, and the classics became "language arts." Similar groupings were also made of the sciences and of the other traditional subjects.

Although these changes had largely originated in the public elementary schools of the 1930s, they soon spread to the public high schools as well. During the later years of the Great Depression the structural and functional characteristics of high schools in the large urban centers of America began to increasingly reflect a grounding in Progressive Education. These high schools were drastically different from not only the private tuition academies but the pre-Depression high schools as well. Some of these new structural and functional characteristics included diversified curriculum, counseling and testing, new teaching methods, flexible standards, extra-curricular activities, milder discipline, and a general sensitivity to the personal as well as the academic needs of the pupils.[29]

New Teacher Preparation Programs

As fundamental beliefs about the value of education were developing in the broader society, they increasingly began to reflect changes in the professional structure of the public high schools. This clearly was evident in the academic credentials that the teachers and administrators were expected to possess. Up to this point they had classical education backgrounds similar to both the teachers in private tuition academies and those in the free public high school era of the late 1800s. But academic requirements for public high school teachers changed significantly after the turn of the century. These new academic requirements, in turn, had a pronounced affect on the structure of the curriculums of colleges and universities, particularly from the 1930s onward. This was especially true for public colleges and universities, since these institutions were subject to the direct political influences of state legislatures.

The task of educating college students to become high school teachers involved having the prospective teachers master the subjects they would be required to teach in the high schools. The subjects that were being taught in the high schools, in turn, had a strong instrumental value, as least as perceived by the teacher educators in the colleges and universities. As a consequence, the subjects, which had their antecedents in the intrinsically valued arts and sciences, clashed with their instrumentally valued equivalents in the core curriculums of many of the new public high schools. In other words, parts of separate and diverse college programs in history, economics, and political science had somehow to be transformed by those in schools of education into a program called "social studies" for the new public high school teachers. The foundation now had been laid for epistemologically grounded conflicts within the university between the faculties of arts and sciences and education. The conflicts were exacerbated when teacher educators argued that teaching methods were at least as important as the content courses in teacher preparation programs in colleges and universities.

The upshot of attempts to resolve these conflicts varied in different institutions of higher education. For instance, in the state teachers colleges the conflicts between the arts and sciences and education was not a major problem. In these institutions, for example, the elementary and secondary school versions of a course in social studies was actually an integral part of the program of the history departments. On the other hand, the history, political science, and economics departments in universities refused to give ground in the matter of an amalgamation of intrinsic content with instrumental methods. Such a demand to amalgamate content and method severely challenged the merit of the intrinsic value they placed on the knowledge of their disciplines and the emphasis placed on the research involved in advancing this knowledge.

Consequently, the teacher-education programs in universities became splintered. For instance, departments of education formerly located in colleges of arts and sciences became separate schools, colleges, and even graduate schools of education.[30] With each successive organizational change these new academic units gained greater autonomy. The outcome was a lessening of the dependence by teacher educators upon traditional academic departments in colleges of arts and sciences.

The major consequence of continual curricular and organizational rearrangements in universities engaged in teacher preparation has been the ever-increasing dominance of the instrumental valuing of knowledge within schools and colleges of education. This is particularly evident in the elementary education departments within schools and colleges of education. These academic departments have their own version of the core content subjects of the arts and sciences. For example, they have curriculum designations in "language arts" instead of English, "social studies" instead of history and the other social sciences, "science education" instead of each of the separate sciences, and "mathematics education" instead of mathematics.[31] On the other hand, teachers preparing to teach in the high schools must take their core subjects in the various academic departments within the arts and sciences. In fact, courses in the arts and sciences generally account for all but a small proportion of the total number of courses that constitute baccalaureate degree programs for aspiring high school teachers. Consequently, future high school teachers, at least those being educated in research-based universities, are more likely to develop an intrinsic value of knowledge --knowledge not justified solely by need and/or use.

The Academic Structures of Schools of Education

The outcome of these conflicts in the valuing of knowledge is fully evident in the academic community, particularly within schools and colleges of education. In this regard the influences of "educational" psychology and its stress on the application of principles of essentially behavioristic psychology to pedagogy, combined with the current emphasis on the classroom "management" aspects of the teaching function, have almost completely overwhelmed the more traditional philosophically based approaches to teacher preparation. To many, this model of teacher preparation reduces teachers to being merely "learning technicians" operating from predetermined scripts.[32]

Other pairings of both real and imagined conflicts in teacher preparation programs also exist within schools of education. These conflicts center around such issues as the theoretical versus the practical dimensions of teaching, the value of philosophical and historical foundations of education versus sociological and anthropological foundations, and the education professor as a university faculty member versus the education professor as a practitioner in the schools. The effects that these conflicts have upon the education of prospective teachers are both manifold and intertwined. Yet conceptually these conflicts can logically be reduced to differences between two fundamental ways to value knowledge, intrinsically and instrumentally.

What makes this conflict in knowledge-valuing complex in any analysis of the academic structures of schools of education is that it constitutes a second-order contradiction, namely an instrumental valuing of knowledge nested within the broader intrinsic/instrumental conflict surrounding teacher preparation in itself. If the functions of schools of education were based conceptually and entirely on a "theory logically guiding practice" process, then this internal contradiction within schools of education is theoretically resolvable. The "theory" dimension of schools of education thus would be the deliberate study of what, how, why, when, and to whom the fundamental knowledge, as found in the arts and sciences, is to be transmitted. The "practice" aspect of schools of education thus would be to prepare future teachers to make decisions about all aspects of their transmitting function in the schools.[33] Granted, this function of a school of education faculty is not the same as that of the arts and sciences faculty--which is discovering and teaching basic knowledge. It is nonetheless an acceptable function in its own right. That function clearly is to assist future teachers in transmitting to the masses the fundamental knowledge encompassed within the academic structures of the arts and sciences.

The Academic Functions of Education Faculties

In one sense, assisting future teachers in transmitting fundamental knowledge could well be interpreted as being instrumental. But, the question here is not whether the teaching of the traditional arts and sciences is more intrinsic than instrumental; rather, it is a question of the degree of instrumental valuing involved. This question can not be answered without first answering at least two basic questions about the intrinsically valued knowledge of the arts and sciences. These questions are: (1) Can the fundamental knowledge of the arts and sciences be understood by the masses? and, if so, then (2) Can it be effectively taught to the masses?

Whether knowledge can be acquired by all, and, if so, taught to all, are questions that take on increasingly complex dimensions within the context of the American system of social justice. For one thing, the states require that every child within a certain age span attend school for the purpose of acquiring an education. On the other hand, states do not require anyone beyond a compulsory school attendance age to be further educated. In this sense, at least, the *modus operandi* of the college/university professor is significantly different from that of the public school teacher. On the one hand, since children are required to attend school by force of law, the public school teacher almost invariably has a "captive" audience. On the other hand, since college students are not required by force of law to attend college, a professor has a "voluntary" audience. Beyond this simple fact all of the other differences between higher education and elementary/secondary education pale in significance.

These differences, although on their face simplistic, nevertheless have a profound effect on the relationship that education faculties have with faculties of other academic units on university campuses. These differences are a major factor in explaining why departments, schools, and colleges of education are generally on the lower level of the academic pecking order within universities yet, once established, are rarely eliminated from the academic structures of universities.[34] In the most negative sense, the inclusion of the field of education within the academic structure of a university can be considered to be politically expedient, and in the most positive sense, a useful adjunct, albeit one of low status. This low status might be a reflection of the diminished value of the teaching function generally held by arts and sciences faculties. This is evident through many of their practices, not the least of which include: (1) the importance placed on the advancement of knowledge as the primary if not sole factor for tenure and promotion; (2) widespread use of graduate assistants, part-time faculty, and new assistant professors for the more undesirable teaching assignments; and, among still others, (3) a discernable lack of interest by the professor-as-teacher in understanding the relationship between teaching and learning.

Teaching Versus Professional Functions

The purpose and function of the public schools strikes at the very heart of the controversy surrounding perspectives of the arts and sciences faculties about the instrumental valuing of knowledge. Through the legislative and/or constitutional mandate of the states, the public schools must first accept *all* children, then do as much as possible to educate them. No matter how intrinsic the knowledge of the subject is perceived to be by the classroom teacher, the teacher still must carry out the state's mandate. They must do this predominantly through the act of teaching the subject for which they are licensed to teach by the state. This places a demand on teachers which is in many ways more complex than that placed upon the arts and sciences professors; yet in other ways it is simpler. More specifically, the teacher is apprised that it is not research and the subsequent enhancement of fundamental knowledge that is valued in state-supported public education. Rather, it is the ability to maximally educate the children through the act of teaching. It is clear, after all, that teachers are almost always hired for their teaching potential. Rarely, if ever, do the public schools employ teachers on the basis of their research and publication record in the subjects they are licensed to teach.

It is in light of the purposes and functions of their respective social institutions that the roles of university professors and public school teachers are clearly differentiated. In universities where the teaching function is highly prized, the faculties are not likely to have a strong reputation as a body of "knowers." On the other hand, those universities considered to be among the leading institutions of higher education in America invariably are not considered to be predominantly "teaching" institutions, regardless of the teaching reputations of their faculties. Clearly, these institutions are more widely recognized for their advancement of fundamental knowledge. Thus, their faculties are not merely strongly encouraged to research; research is actually demanded of them as a condition for initial employment, the gaining of tenure, academic promotions, and salary increases. Even in those colleges and universities that highly prize and might even be widely known for their teaching, the concept of the professor as a "knower" generally prevails.

In order to more fully understand the fundamental relationship of the field of education to the university, the primary function of the professor, on the one hand, and the elementary and secondary school teacher, on the other, demands clarification. It is indeed the single most important factor inherent in the teacher-education controversy. But the question here is not whether differences exist between the functions of public school teachers and professors, for it is clear that they do. Furthermore, college and university professors cannot have their essential functions so altered that they will more approximate those of public school teachers. To do that, even if it were possible, would be tantamount to contradicting the intrinsic valuing of knowledge that promotes the possibility of an infinite rationality.[35] For it is the desire to pursue knowledge for its own sake that the faculties of colleges of arts and sciences serve as the paradigm for all professors. Thus, the fundamental questions in the teacher-preparation controversy that need clarification are, "What is the function of a school of education within the structure of a university?" and "What is the role of the professor of education within the university setting?"

3. Teacher Education and Higher Education

During most of the nineteenth century many public school teachers were prepared in private normal schools, the first being founded in 1823 by the Reverend Samuel R. Hall.[36] The curriculum of these early normal schools focused exclusively on "schoolkeeping" to prospective teachers.[37] Because of the demand for trained teachers for the rapidly increasing number of public common schools being started at this time, the normal school approach to teacher preparation increased both quantitatively and qualitatively. But the private normal schools simply could not meet the demand for the number of trained teachers needed for the rapidly growing public schools. To meet this pressing need for teachers, numerous public normal schools were operating by the turn of the twentieth century.[38]

After the turn of the century, many of the larger state-supported public normal schools were transformed into state "teachers colleges." Concurrent with this transformation, a great need developed for teachers to staff the burgeoning number of new public high schools. The private tuition academies and the colleges of arts and letters in universities could not prepare sufficient numbers of teachers to meet this need. For this reason, as well as a variety of economic, political, geographic, and demographic factors, state teachers colleges began to merge their preparation programs for grammar school teachers (now more commonly called "elementary" school teachers) with programs to prepare high school teachers. Simultaneously, these new state teachers colleges began to increasingly acquire not only the characteristics of a traditional four-year college, but in some instances they began to take on characteristics of university colleges of arts and sciences.[39] With teacher education institutionalized in higher education, the stage was now set for the conflict in the intrinsic/instrumental valuing of knowledge in teacher preparation.

Criticisms of the Free Public High School

The conflict between the intrinsic versus the instrumental valuing of knowledge in public education began to manifest itself in at least two settings, in the new public high schools and the colleges and universities which the graduates of these new high schools would be attending. Some new public high schools, now increasingly being staffed by teachers that were not prepared in the classical tradition, were located in fashionable parts of big cities and their adjacent upward-mobile suburbs. The parents of the students in these high schools quite naturally expected their children to receive a high school education that would enable them to succeed in college. But the traditional colleges and universities that these students would be attending were neither accustomed nor prepared for the type of student coming from the new free public high schools. This was particularly true of schools that were staffed by a new breed of teachers coming from the new state teachers colleges.

Up to this time, the institutions of higher education had been enrolling a specific type of college student. These students invariably had been taught by teachers possessing the then traditional "arts baccalaureate" degree. Such teachers were more likely to be found in the private tuition academies which were popular during much of the nineteenth century. But students graduating from the newer and more numerous free public high schools often failed to meet the academic standards of the more prestigious colleges and universities. As a result, questions were raised about the quality of a public high school education. Whether grounded in fact or supposition, these criticisms began to have a pronounced influence on the curriculum and teaching methods then prevailing in the public high schools.

Invariably, other factors also brought about increased criticisms of the public high schools. The criticisms were directed at virtually all facets of the academic structure of these institutions, but more than anything else they focused on the methods of teaching. The criticisms ranged from direct overt and often vitriolic condemnations to subtle innuendo; however, these criticisms rarely took into consideration the stated philosophy and objectives of the school systems or legitimate empirical evidence. Rather, the critics assailed many of the teaching practices and curricular programs as simply novelty, administrative expedience, political bargaining, or some combination of these.

For example, critics claimed that the failure of a high school student to be admitted to a college was due to either an "outdated" high school program, or, conversely, the school's attempts to be current by adopting poorly conceived and novel changes in its curriculum. Some critics claimed that many of the courses in the high schools were seriously "out of date." On the other hand, when new courses were added to the high school curriculum and the students still failed to be admitted to college, then the "newness" of the courses was faulted. In other words, either tradition, novelty, or a combination of these criticisms was used to explain a student's academic failure in college. In most cases teachers, principals, and school boards could do little but simply bear the brunt of these attacks on their educational expertise.

On the other hand, for some schools the charges of the critics were credible. These schools indeed dealt with the alleged shortcomings through administrative contrivances at the school level or expedient political processes at the district level. Sometimes novel school programs and their concomitant changes in administrative procedures gave the impression that the fundamental curriculum changes demanded by the critics actually had been made. Changes in administrative procedures included standardizing the time spent in class, establishing unified grading procedures, and more closely evaluating teaching methods. Politically, boards of education often would succumb to the source of greatest pressure emanating from the local critics. If, for example, influential people in the community were disappointed because local high school graduates were not being admitted to colleges and universities, then the school board likely would be pressured to look more closely at the academic program of the high school. This included close scrutiny of the teaching practices in terms of tradition, novelty, and administrative procedures and structure.

But, by and large, the responses of the public high school policy-makers to the growing number of high school graduates having their university and college ambitions frustrated were not grounded in any theory-logically-guiding-practice strategy. Instead, their policies were often inconsistent with just *what* significantly affected a student's entrance to and eventual success in college. Either the policy-makers were unenlightened regarding the basic nature of just what significantly affected success in college or, for political reasons, they ignored such information if, in fact, it was available. Clearly, in retrospect at least, the roots of the problem were the fundamental changes in the structure of the American society in general, and, in particular, the institutional structure of the evolving free public high school.

Environmental Press for Changes in Teacher Preparation

By the turn of the twentieth century the American society clearly had become more industrial rather than agricultural. Parallel to this fundamental structural change in the American society, the public schools, through consolidation, were becoming more centralized.[40] Increasingly, many of the newer consolidated schools reflected the values of a much broader and subsequently more complex community instead of the values of the smaller and more homogeneous immediate community in which they existed. This new era of the public school in America can appropriately be called the "school of the lost community." What was lacking in their transition from small local schools to larger more cosmopolitan ones was as manifold as it was varied in origin.

In the new larger high schools the students were now being exposed to the many different values and cultures of not only their fellow students but the teachers as well. The wider range of values from teachers came from at least two important sources. One was the ever-growing number of high school teachers that were graduating from the new state teachers colleges. Although the teachers colleges were not entirely like those of the liberal arts colleges and universities which emphasized the broad liberal arts as the core of their academic structure, the teachers colleges nevertheless required students to take many courses in the liberal arts and sciences.[41]

A second source contributing to a wider range of values likewise came from the teachers colleges. In the 1930s and 1940s, teachers colleges increasingly were being staffed by graduates from such prestigious teacher-education institutions as Teachers College, Columbia University, and George Peabody College. Many professors of education in these and similar institutions were imbued with the philosophy and techniques of "Progressive Education," which emphasized the importance of individual values. Because of their reputation, these institutions attracted comparatively large numbers of prospective teachers. Coming from virtually all parts of the country, they brought with them not only their various values but other elements of their cultures as well. When they left as elementary or high school teachers, they took home with them a newly acquired cosmopolitan perspective which they passed on to many of their students.

Preparation Programs for High School Teachers

Due to the press for staffing the many new free public high schools coming into existence, demands were placed on the states to increase their financial support of teacher preparation for the secondary schools. But the states found it difficult, if not impossible in some cases, to get the more traditional state-supported universities to help meet the need to prepare more high school teachers. This was largely due to the resistance of the arts and sciences faculties in these universities and the low regard that most academics had for teacher education. As a consequence, external political pressures led to funding the formation of departments and schools of education within state supported universities.[42] But this effort to prepare more high school teachers was bound to frustration.

Early in their history departments of education in universities were usually staffed by those faculty members of the college of arts and sciences who were less inclined to continue the research tradition inherent in the arts and sciences. Whatever such personal motives might have been, the academic units initially associated with the process of developing separate departments of education often were the departments of psychology and philosophy.[43] Consequently, the many specific teaching fields of the prospective high school teachers were not the focus of the curriculums being developed by these new departments of education. For example, if a student majoring in mathematics, a science, or history planned to teach in a high school, then the student was required to "major" in that respective area in the college of arts and sciences. In terms of subject matter, the future high school teacher was to be treated academically the same as the prospective mathematician, scientist, or historian.[44] This presented a number of problems for schools of education that were trying to attract more students to their high school teacher preparation programs. One such problem was economic in nature and was beyond the control of the universities.

The salaries of graduates in the arts and sciences who pursued teaching careers at the high school level were generally lower than those of other graduates. Low salaries thus became a major deterrent for attracting many quality students to the teacher education programs of a university's college of arts and sciences. Obstacles in the public schools, other than those of salary, also served to suppress the number of university and college students preparing to be teachers. These factors included a perceived lack of autonomy, excessive administrative control, continual parental criticism, and community-enforced rigid moral standards. Although state governments had little or no control over personal esteem and societal factors, they could, to a large degree, control the economic factor.

State Reactions to Environmental Press for Change

The already existing normal schools and teachers colleges were the avenues of least resistance open to the states for massively increasing the number of available high school teachers. As a consequence, the states mandated changes in the purposes, functions, structures, and finances of these institutions. In some instances normal schools were virtually legislated into being colleges or were integrated with existing teachers colleges. Subsequently, many of these institutions were thus transformed into institutions that prepared secondary school teachers as well as elementary teachers. In most instances, the elementary education programs in these institutions were left intact; however, secondary teacher education programs began to receive an increasing share of the teacher-preparation resources. But the changes in the purpose, function, structure, and finances of these institutions were not commensurate with the changes in the views of their faculties. This was so because the programs needed to prepare high school teachers were in serious conflict with the existing academic structures and functions of many of these institutions. The outcome was that the fundamental changes in the academic structures needed to effectively prepare high school teachers in these institutions never were fully institutionalized. Thus the changes made in these institutions were more cosmetic than real.

One example of this was that some state teachers colleges, in order to gain respectability, reorganized their academic structures to reflect that of the more traditional liberal arts college.[45] While retaining their emphasis on education and pedagogy, these teachers colleges created their own departments of science and humanities, among perhaps others. Yet these teachers colleges rarely included new faculty members in their newly created departments of science and humanaties with an academic preparation parallel to that of the respective academic faculties in a university college of arts and sciences. Rather, these teachers colleges-turned-pseudo-"liberal arts"-colleges often recast professors of "education" into the roles of professors of "education *and* natural science," professors of "education *and* humanities," or the like. These transformations of roles were often done merely by administrative fiat.

This mirroring of the traditional arts and sciences academic structure subsequently conveyed the false image that a traditional academic major, like those offered by universities, could now be acquired at what was still essentially a teachers college.

The next stage in the development of the secondary teacher-preparation function of former normal schools-turned-state teachers colleges was even more noteworthy in its cosmetic effects. This was especially evident in states that, through legislative fiat, removed the word "teachers" from the title, "state teachers college," and simply gave them the title, "state college." This was done with little or no consideration as to whether those institutions had the ability to reflect an academic nature commensurate with the traditional concept of a liberal arts or comprehensive college. Nevertheless, the transformation process of the state normal schools and state teachers colleges was almost complete. The last step was to bestow on them the title "university" and the metamorphosis would be complete.

At the present time, the number of state colleges has diminished because they in fact have been officially designated as "state universities." It should be reiterated that this transformation from state normal schools and teachers colleges to state universities had not automatically infused these institutions with the ideals of the traditional university. Initially, at least, the faculties of these institutions did not necessarily have the same academic background or interests as did those of arts and sciences faculties in traditional universities. In addition, the graduate school programs within these transformed normal schools/teachers colleges also differed widely from those in traditional universities. The granting of many kinds of master and doctoral degrees was very limited in most of these new institutions when compared to that of traditional universities. It should also be noted that the teacher preparation function of these newly created "universities" still prevails in the 1980s.

Teacher Education Conflicts in Traditional Universities

In traditional universities, serious conflicts evolved between newly established departments of education and some of the more traditional academic departments. Differences in fundamental beliefs about education lay at the roots of these conflicts. Professors in other departments, such as psychology and philosophy, who had joint appointments in departments of education, often found themselves in the middle of these conflicts. Likewise, so were many of the new or junior members of traditional academic departments who were sometimes required to teach courses in the teacher preparation programs. Compounding these forced interactions between departments of education and other academic departments were: (1) state mandates for increased teacher preparation facilities, (2) motives and ideals of new members of education departments, (3) demands of students wanting to teach in the public schools, and (4) arts and sciences faculties applying their standards of research and publication for tenure and promotion to the faculties of the newly created education departments. A major consequence of these pressures was the complete transfer of the teacher preparation function, as overseen by departments of education formerly in colleges of arts and sciences, to largely autonomous schools or colleges of education.

Thus, the shift from the intrinsic to the largely instrumental valuing of knowledge in the field of education can be seen in the transformation of state normal schools and state teachers colleges first into state colleges and then into state universities. Within traditional research-based universities, the differences between colleges of arts and sciences and schools of education are more explicit. This is due in large part to their organizational relationship within the university. As previously noted and discussed, one of the major consequences of this academic restructuring is the fact that schools of education are usually viewed as being at the low end of the academic spectrum. This can be largely explained by schools of education valuing knowledge instrumentally. This, of course, is contrary to the traditional arts and sciences academic influence within universities; namely, that of valuing knowledge intrinsically.

Notwithstanding the increasing numbers of professional school graduates, the intrinsic valuing of knowledge still prevails over the instrumental valuing of knowledge in most research-based universities. In addition, the problems surrounding schools of education within universities are further exacerbated by the differing demands of society and the university. On the one hand, society generally expects that professors of education should exhibit an instrumental valuing of knowledge because they "teach teachers *how* to teach." On the other hand, the academic community of the university expects professors of education to demonstrate that they value knowledge intrinsically because the university ideal requires that all professors engage in research. In the case of the education professor, that research should be into any and all aspects of the deliberate transmission of the liberal arts and sciences to the masses. The contradictions between the expectations of the broader society and those of the university community for the role of professors of education creates serious dilemmas for all involved. For professors of education, at least, their role can best be described as being academically schizophrenic.

NOTES

1. The reader is reminded that it is not the intention of the authors to fully detail all aspects of the history surrounding the basic elements of the analysis and critique that are the focus of this book. There is a plethora of historical references that could be listed here and in other sections. For a brief but excellent reference for the non-historian, see James Burke, *The Day the Universe Changed* (Boston: Little, Brown and Company, 1985).

2. For a brief discussion of the contributions of Aquinas to realism, see Hobert W. Burns and Charles J. Brauner, *Philosophy of Education: Essays and Commentaries* (New York: The Ronald Press, 1962), pp. 96-98.

3. For an interesting discussion of the contributions of Roger Bacon to scientific thought, see Malachi Martin, "The Insignificant Cry of Roger Bacon," *Intellectual Digest* (August 1972): 52-55.

4. See Edgar Knight, *Twenty Centuries of Education* (Boston: Ginn, 1940), as cited in Charles J. Fazzaro, "Four Myths of the American University and Their Influences on Its Development," *Social Science* (Summer 1976): 140.

5. For a more complete discussion of this aspect of the medieval scholars, see Eric Ashby, "Second Edition/The University Ideal," *The Center Magazine* (January/February 1973): 37-41.

6. For an example of a political perspective of university governance, see J. Victor Baldridge, *Power and Conflict in the University* (New York: John Wiley and Sons, 1971). Also, for an interesting analysis--based on the work of late French scholar Michel Foucault--of the increasing political intervention of state governments into the affairs of universities and colleges, see Richard A. Hartnett, "The Pastoral Power of the State and the Autonomy of Higher Education" (Paper delivered at the O.I.S.E. Conference on Governments and Higher Education, London, 23 October 1986).

7. An earlier reference to a dichotomy between the intrinsic and the instrumental valuing of knowledge was introduced by Charles J. Brauner and Hobert W. Burns. In this regard they said: "In all fairness, the issue is not whether a student should have at his command a fund of information, a collection of related facts, or an understanding of a body of knowledge--for even the most progressive educators would agree to that. The issue is whether such a fund of information is an end in and of itself or whether it is a means to the end of successful human activity; *the issue is whether knowledge is of intrinsic or instrumental value* (emphasis added)." See Charles J. Brauner and Hobert W. Burns, *Problems in Philosophy of Education* (Englewood Cliffs, New Jersey: Prentice Hall, 1965), p. 38.

8. For an analysis of the effects of vocationalism on the academic structures of universities, see Henry R. Weinstock, "A Critique of Criticisms of Vocationalism," *The Educational Forum* 32, no. 2 (January 1968): 165-69.

9. In 1970-71 there were 418,583 bachelor's degrees awarded in the Arts and Sciences and 421,147 in technical and professional fields. By 1984-85 these figures had changed to 340,800 and 638,677 respectively. Thus, in 1970-71 arts and sciences made up about 50 percent of all bachelor's degrees conferred by American colleges and universities. By 1984-85 this had declined to about 35 percent. On the other hand, the number of technical/professional degrees increased by 52 percent, accounting for nearly two-thirds of all bachelor's degrees awarded in 1984-85. See Joyce D. Stern (ed.), *The Condition of Education* (Washington, D.C.: U.S. Government Printing Office, 1987), p. 104.

10. In almost every instance the starting salaries for assistant professors in professional schools, such as law and business administration, are *significantly* higher than starting salaries in the liberal arts and sciences. For example, for the 1986-87 academic year the average starting salary of an assistant professor in Law was $38,293 and for Business it was $38,017. On the other hand, it was $27,413 for the Physical Sciences and only $22,839 for Fine Arts. See "Two Steps Forward...?" The Annual Report on the Economic Status of the Profession, 1986-87, *Academe* 73, no. 2 (March-April 1987): 6.

11. It should be noted that many of the various academic departments in the sciences have fared comparatively very well financially since at least the 1950s. This is a result of dramatic increases in federal grants to scientists within universities. Much of this money was intended for research directly related to national defense and space exploration.

12. The use of the term "practical" in this context is not to be confused with Aristotle's "practical" wisdom, which is discussed later. Instead, the term "practical" as used here carries the more popular definition, "useful."

13. See Theodore R. Crane, ed., *The College and the Public 1787-1862* (New York: Columbia University Press, 1963).

14. See George L. Newsome, Jr., "American University Patterns, 1776-1900: A Study of Six Selected Universities" (Ph.D. diss., Yale University, 1956), p. 119.

15. For further treatment of this, see Henry R. Weinstock, "An Analysis of Issues in Liberal and Professional Undergraduate Education" (Ed.D. diss., University of Georgia, Athens, 1965), p. 43.

16. Although the sciences are treated here as being part of the central core of the university, it should be noted that they came to be recognized as part of the central core only within the last one hundred years or so. Originally, the central core was composed of the "arts and letters" and not the sciences.

17. Colleges of "arts and sciences" emerged in American universities shortly after the Civil War period when colleges of "liberal arts" began to lose their prominence in the academic structure. This was a consequence of universities evolving into complex administrative units that included graduate, professional, and collegiate schools. See Weinstock, *op. cit.*, p. 51.

18. For a full discussion of the history of electrical engineering in the university, see Robert Rosenberg, "American Physics and the Origins of Electrical Engineering," *Physics Today* 36, no. 10 (October 1983): 48-54.

19. See Clarence Stephen Marsh, "Business Education at the College Level," *American Council on Educational Studies*, no. 7 (March 1934): 8.

20. By 1900, there were seven institutions of higher education giving collegiate instruction in business. These included those at the University of Chicago (1898), University of California (1898), University of Wisconsin (1900), Dartmouth College (1900), and New York University (1900). Soon after, in 1908, the first university school of journalism was started at the University of Missouri. This particular professional program apparently grew out of a six-year extended course started some thirty years earlier. See Weinstock, *op. cit.*, pp. 95 and 106.

21. According to Blocker, *et al.*, "These early colleges were true extensions of secondary education; they were housed in high school buildings, had closely articulated curricula, and shared faculty and administrative staff." See Clyde E. Blocker, Robert H. Plummer, and Richard C. Richardson, Jr., *The Two-Year College: A Social Synthesis* (Englewood Cliffs, New Jersey: Prentice-Hall, 1965), p. 25.

22. For a more in-depth discussion of the relationship of schools of education to colleges of arts and sciences, see Henry R. Weinstock, "Comparing a School of Education to a College of Arts and Sciences and Professional Schools in a University," *Proceedings of the Southwestern Philosophy of Education Society* 33 (1983): 159-64.

23. Price comments that, "*Education* means the academic discipline which attempts to understand the deliberate process of bequeathing and improving the arts and sciences. And this discipline consists of a certain set of facts drawn from many sources as well as a set of recommendations based upon them as to the way in which this process may be most usefully dispatched." See Kingsley Price, "What is a Philosophy of Education?" *Educational Theory* 6 (April 1956): 86-94.

24. In Massachusetts in the early 1820s, the president of Amherst College commented that on the annual reports from school committees there were many complaints about the quality of teachers in the schools. He said that, "I might quote their complaints till sunset, that it is impossible to have good schools for want of good teachers. Many who offer themselves are deficient in everything; in spelling, in reading, in penmanship, in geography, in grammar, and in common arithmetic. The majority would be dismissed and advised to go back to their domestic and rural employments, if competent instructors could be had." See Charles A. Harper, *A Century of Public Teacher Education* (Washington, D.C.: American Association of Teachers Colleges, 1939), pp. 12-13.

25. As early as 1825 it was evident that in many parts of the United States there was a dissatisfaction with the quality of teachers in the developing system of grammar schools. In that same year James G. Carter published an article in the *Boston Patriot* calling for the passage of an act of the state legislature for a state-supported normal school. Because of his persistence he has been given the title of "Father of the American Normal School." See Harper, pp. 15-16.

26. There were just over 2,500 high schools in 1890, with a total enrollment of over 200,000. By 1910, only twenty years later, there were well over 10,000 high schools, with a pupil enrollment of more than 900,000. See John S. Brubacher, *A History of the Problems of Education* (New York: McGraw-Hill, 1937), p. 435.

27. In 1850 there were about 6,000 tuition academies and only a few free public high schools in the United States. By 1900 the number of tuition academies had dropped to about 1,200, whereas the number of free public high schools had increased to about 6,000. See Ellwood P. Cubberley, *Public Education in the United States* (Boston: Houghton Mifflin, 1934), p. 255.

28. By 1900 there were at least four normal schools in the United States that truly could be called teacher colleges. By the 1940s there were close to one hundred fifty degree-conferring state teachers colleges, some offering graduate work. See Harper, p. 133.

29. See David Swift, *Ideology and Change in the Public Schools* (Columbus, Ohio: Merrill, 1971), pp. 31-64.

30. For an example of how this conflict was resolved in at least one university, the University of Pennsylvania, see David A. Goddard, "The College of Education Within the University," in *The Role of the College of Education Within the University*, ed. Anthony Scarangello (Newark, Delaware: College of Education, 1969), pp. 51-59.

31. An example of a current criticism of this arrangement is that of President Reagan's Commission on Excellence in Education. The Commission reported that, "The teacher preparation curriculum is weighted heavily with courses in educational methods at the expense of courses in subjects to be taught. A survey of 1,350 institutions training teachers indicated that 41 percent of the time of elementary-school teacher candidates is spent in education courses, which reduces the amount of time available for subject-matter courses." See National Commission on Excellence in Education, "An Open Letter to the American People, 'A Nation at Risk: The Imperative for Educational Reform,'" *Education Week* (27 April 1983): 14.

32. For a particularly interesting discussion of this "scientific" approach to teaching, see Wilfred Carr and Stephen Kemmis, *Becoming Critical: Education, Knowledge and Action Research* (Philadelphia: The Falmer Press, 1986), pp. 61-70.

33. Harold Taylor, a former president of Sarah Lawrence College, gave this view of the role of a college of education in a university: "The college of education needs poets, sculptors, anthropologists, who are concerned about the character of the society here and abroad; psychologists who are interested in students and how they grow; historians who are involved with the cultural history of the United States and of the world society. The educational system has within it the stuff of human life. A serious scholar attached to a college of education can find there a glorious opportunity for considering the problems of contemporary man, or the problems of man through history. A direct confrontation with an educational system is an exercise in the practical application of philosophy, a means of searching for historical truth. The college of education should be a place where scholars and teachers join together to *find insights into the means through which man has come to be what he is* (emphasis added)." See Harold Taylor, "The University as an Instrument of Change," in *The Role of the College of Education Within the University*,

ed. Anthony Scarangello (Newark, Delaware: College of Education, 1969), pp. 48-49.

34. See Goddard, pp. 51-52.

35. The concept of "rationality" was introduced by Max Weber to define bureaucratic decision-making and authority in capitalistic economic systems. This he viewed as purposive-rational action. On the other hand, Herbert Marcuse took Weber's formal concept of "rationality" and considered its implications for the broader society. Marcuse believed that rationality was a specific form of political domination by removing the "total social framework of interests in which strategies are chosen, technologies applied, and systems established from the scope of reflection and rational reconstruction." See Jurgen Habermas, *Toward a Rational Society* (Boston: Beacon Press, 1968), pp. 81-82. For the purposes of the discussion herein, the meaning of rationality goes beyond Weber's narrow sense of the term--that rationality is predicated solely on the criteria of technology and science--to include *all* possible ways of knowing, whatever they might be or can be. Also, rationality as used here is assumed to be a sociopsychological construct made up of mental acts (cognitive processes) mediated through social acts (environmental interactions). See Charles J. Fazzaro, "The U.S. Constitution as a Philosophy of Education: Implications for Rationality and Legitimacy," *Proceedings of the Southwestern Philosophy of Education Society* 37 (1987): 103.

36. Hall opened his private academy for the preparation of teachers in Concord, Vermont in 1823. Although he had only a few students when his school first opened, his views on teacher preparation gained a considerable reputation. In fact, soon after he opened his school he published his *Lectures on Schoolkeeping*, which was used in the normal schools in Massachusetts, New York, Michigan, and Illinois in the 1840s and 1850s. See Harper, p. 13.

37. It is interesting to note that Hall organized the curriculum of his school entirely on the basis of his own observations and experiences and not on the basis of any then known "theories" of education. See Cubberley, p. 375.

38. On July 3, 1839, the first state normal school opened in Lexington, Massachusetts, with three women in attendance. By 1939, there were over 100,000 students enrolled in two hundred teachers colleges throughout the country. See Harper, p. 7.

39. It should be noted that some state teachers colleges that began their existence as normal schools even discontinued their preparation programs for elementary teachers. This was a result of these institutions raising their entrance requirements to correspond to those of other "eastern colleges in

good standing" and requiring a high school diploma for entrance. See Harper, pp. 136-37.

40. From the turn of the twentieth century until about 1970 the consolidation of school districts had been very dramatic. The number of districts dropped from several hundred thousand in 1900 to about 127,000 in 1931 to only about 18,000 in 1970. Although the number of school districts were declining sharply during this period, the number of high schools increased until about 1956, then declined only moderately thereafter. For example, in 1890 there were only about 2500 high schools with a total enrollment of about 200,000, but by 1900 there were over 10,000 with more than 900,000 students enrolled. The growth in the number of high schools continued, but not in proportion with the growth in the numbers of students. For example, in 1931 there were about 26,000 high schools in the United States enrolling several million students. On the other hand, in 1986 there were still more than 23,000 high schools but with a total enrollment of about 12 million students. During this fifty-five year period the average high school was clearly becoming much larger. See Stephen J. Knezevich, *Administration of Public Education* (New York: Harper & Row, 1984), pp. 173 and 330. The increases in both the total number of high schools and the numbers of students they enrolled can be explained by the growing importance of the high school as a significant social institution in the fabric of American society.

41. Early in their development, teachers colleges took two routes in order to achieve status and recognition. One was to adopt the academic standards of the traditional liberal arts college; the second was to set up and enforce their own standards. See Harper, pp. 142-43.

42. By 1910, several Middle Western state universities had changed their departments of education into separate schools of education. See Henry R. Weinstock, "An Analysis of Issues in Liberal and Professional Undergraduate Education," pp. 86-87.

43. In most universities, "colleges" of education grew out of "departments" of education which, in turn, were often developed from already existing departments of psychology and philosophy. See Weinstock, "An Analysis of Issues in Liberal and Professional Undergraduate Education," p. 91.

44. The situation was more critical for prospective elementary teachers because there was no specific "major" for them in existing university undergraduate programs. See Weinstock, "An Analysis of Issues in Liberal and Professional Undergraduate Education," p. 91.

45. According to Armentraut, "Many teachers colleges in their desire to achieve respectability have initiated the patterns and methods of the traditional liberal arts college. . . ." See W. D. Armentraut, "The Teacher College," in *The American College*, ed. P. F. Valentine (New York: Philosophical Library, 1949), pp. 229-30.

Two

The Valuing of Knowledge
in Transition

Overview

The shift from a fundamentally intrinsic to a fundamentally instrumental valuing of knowledge in the broader society took place over many
centuries. This shift was a result of a web of complex and interwoven factors
too numerous to fully explicate in this discussion. What will be examined here
are the roles of American universities and public education in this transition.
These roles were interlocked at several levels as a result of societal forces
external to these institutions. For example, the severe shortage of teachers for
the rapidly increasing number of public schools in the late nineteenth century
brought pressures on universities to incorporate "teacher education" into their
academic structures. For various epistemological, organizational, and
administrative reasons universities soon found it necessary to include within
their faculty structures a new sub-structure, the "education" professoriate. But
because of the developing nature of teacher education, the incorporation of
the education professoriate soon led to contradictions between the institutional and societal views of the role of this new academic sub-structure. On
the one hand, the idealized institutional role of the university professoriate was
that of advancing knowledge through "scholarly inquiry," a view that was
particularly strong in the liberal arts and sciences. On the other hand, the
societal-idealized role of the new education professoriate was that of teaching
the "practical" applications of pedagogy to aspiring school teachers. Thus, to
be able to function effectively, the education professors had to deal with the

contradictions inherent between their institutionally idealized and societally perceived roles.

At about the time that teacher education was being incorporated into the university structure, many new professional schools were also being added. This compounded and sharpened the academic/territorial and other political conflicts that arose between the arts and sciences and the new academic sub-structures. These conflicts clearly were rooted in their respective differences in the valuing of knowledge. On the one hand, the liberal arts and sciences, by seeking "truth" through scholarly inquiry, continued to foster the centuries-old university tradition of valuing knowledge intrinsically. On the other hand, the new professional schools began to establish a tradition of valuing knowledge instrumentally. They did this by "picking and choosing" from the arts and sciences only that knowledge which they perceived to be important for the practices inherent in their respective professions.

Education professors soon found themselves in a novel and inherently contradictory position with the arts and sciences tradition. Within universities, at least, professors of education were required to (1) know the knowledge embodied in the arts and sciences so that they could (2) recommend to aspiring public school teachers how to teach this knowledge to the masses. Thus, schools of education and their professoriates were concurrently immersed in the functional aspects of two institutions, the university and the public schools--both educational in nature, but each unique in character and in the role society expected them to fulfill.

Although the societal view of the university can be analyzed at several levels, at its most simplistic form the analysis can be done by contrasting the role of the university to that of the public schools. Whereas both of these institutions involve knowledge and its transmission, the knowledge taught by teachers in the public schools is generally considered to be of lower scholarly worth than the knowledge within the academic structures of universities. Another significant difference lies in the fact that a student can select, then, at least, attempt to gain knowledge inherent in the university, and attendance is only *voluntary*. In contrast, the knowledge choices for students in the public schools are either non-existent or very limited at best, and attendance is *mandatory*, at least up to a legally established age.

But structural changes in society, particularly after WWII, not only raised the educational requisites for entrance into many professions but also the educational aspirations of virtually everyone in the rapidly growing middle classes. Over a relatively short time, a college or university degree became a virtual requirement for many jobs. Requiring more years of formal education for increasingly greater numbers of jobs brought pressures on universities to vastly expand their academic programs and enrollments. As universities grew rapidly they significantly expanded their management *qua* administrative structures. This, in turn, dramatically changed their governance structure from the traditional collegial/political to one best described as being bureaucratic/rational-technical. These changes in the management and governance structures of universities had direct implications for the fundamental transformation of their academic structures.

The development of large, rationalized bureaucratic organizations, particularly business organizations, within the broader society further strengthened the general belief that bureaucratic structures and processes were in fact superior for *all* organizations, regardless of their fundamental nature. For at least two important reasons this growing belief in the superiority of bureaucracy further sharpened the contradictions between societal expectations of the university and the traditional academic structures within the university. First, many universities adopted business management philosophies and techniques, regardless of the contradictions between both the bureaucratic structures and production functions of businesses and the traditional collegial structures and educational functions of universities. Secondly, the instrumental knowledge demands of the professions, business, and the corporate world forced universities to increasingly accommodate into their academic structures greater numbers of professors who, contrary to the traditional university ideal, valued knowledge more instrumentally.

But in order to survive as legitimate and viable educational institutions in the ideal American democracy, universities cannot be burdened by rigid bureaucratic structures. Unencumbered by the inflexibilities inherent in all bureaucracies, universities, in their continual search for "truth," would be able to more freely accommodate a potentially infinite array of rationalities. But regardless of how societal beliefs about organizations influence the management, governance, and academic structures of universities, the heightened valuing of knowledge conflicts between diverse academic units--colleges of arts and sciences, professional schools, and the schools of education--impedes any progress that universities might make in freeing themselves from the bonds of bureaucracy. To better understand these valuing of knowledge conflicts and their educational implications it is first necessary to have an understanding of the unique roles and functions of the diverse academic units within the structures of modern American universities.

4. Valuing Knowledge and the Evolving Education Professoriate

The role of the field of education within the academic structure of traditional universities has always been replete with contradictions, particularly for education professors. These contradictions are rooted primarily in the rational myths surrounding the role of the arts and sciences professoriates and are revealed in the status of both the field of education and the education professoriate within university academic communities. For example, students who major in education have low academic status due in part to the prevailing myth on most university campuses that these students do not do as well in arts and sciences courses as students pursuing an arts and sciences degree.[1] Likewise, education professors have low academic status because most courses taught by professors of education are generally considered to have little or no academic rigor. True, there are other academic units within universities that historically have had low academic status, but low academic status is especially crucial for the field of education. This is so because theoretically, at least, the field of education should be closer to colleges of arts and sciences than any other academic unit in the university. After all, it is the knowledge represented in the college of arts and sciences that public school teachers are expected to teach to the masses.

Perhaps the factor that contributes most to the low academic status of professors of education within the university communities is the lack of clarity about their *modus operandi*. On the one hand, in order for university professors to achieve promotion in rank and eventually tenure they must demonstrate through their basic research that they have advanced knowledge within an academic field of study. But in the field of education there is a constant hue and cry from society generally and public school teachers and administrators in particular for "practical" application of knowledge about *how* to educate children in the public schools setting. Thus, "practical" or applied research is viewed by many education professors as being more important than basic research. The upshot of this is that the applied research of education professors, as well as that in many other newly developed "professional" schools, generally is given a somewhat diminished status in universities.

On the other hand, there might be some justification for demanding "practical" relevance from the research conducted by professors of education. At the pragmatic level, for example, it is likely that if education professors engaged in only basic research, then the broader society would have a somewhat lesser view of their *raison d'être*. But upon further analysis, neither basic nor applied research should be considered mutually exclusive activities for professors of education. This is particularly true for education professors in modern research-based universities where academic standing is directly related to research activities.

Although many academic traditionalists in universities believe that *any* research about education is not worthy of scholarly status, the sheer volume of the research by education professors, regardless of its character and perceived quality, has helped the field of education to enhance its academic standing. More specifically, even the research of education professors who do purely "professional" or applied research is viewed more favorably by the academic traditionalists than no research at all. The status of this kind of research is enhanced even further if the research is comprehensive and systematic and based on theoretical, logical, and factual principles. But the devaluing of basic research by education professors simply because society more highly values the pedagogical aspects of education (*qua* applied research) has not been viewed as a defensible position by the traditional university professoriates.

Thus, the important issues with which education professors must contend are (1) the contradictions inherent in the fundamental differences between basic and applied research and (2) the differences between societal expectations and university expectations for their role in the university. How these issues are dealt with ultimately affects the status of the education professor. Also, as previously noted, the status of the education professoriate is low for two other important reasons. First, the traditional university professoriate has not considered the teaching of simply *how* to teach to be a legitimate academic endeavor. Secondly, applied research (which is a manifestation of an instrumental valuing of knowledge) has generally been accorded low status by the traditional arts and sciences professoriates. Thus, by largely limiting its *modus operandi* to teaching prospective public school teachers *how* to teach and *not* emphasizing basic research (a manifestation of an intrinsic valuing of knowledge), the education professoriate is a fundamental contradiction to the traditional university ideal inherent in the arts and sciences professoriates.

Knowledge and the University

The intrinsic/instrumental model for valuing knowledge is useful for clarifying what has been at stake historically in the seemingly irresolvable contradictions confronting the field of education within universities. One place to begin such a clarification lies within the fundamental concepts of knowledge which had become the epistemological foundations of the disciplines found in traditional universities. The bases for these epistemological foundations are the contradictory explanations of reality grounded in the Formal Idealism of Plato (427-347 B.C.) and the Classical Realism of Aristotle (384-322 B.C.). Later, scholars such as John Locke (1632-1704) and Immanuel Kant (1724-1804), each in his own way, took elements of idealism and realism and modified them into the philosophical perspectives that are the epistemological foundations of many of the academic disciplines in modern universities. For those who are not entirely familiar with the nature and history of these distinctly different worldviews a brief review is in order.

Plato's Formal Idealism. Plato had averred that the world of human experience can be likened to the ebb and flow of the tides--the tides wash in and the tides wash out. The resulting lack of permanence that Plato attributed to reality was similar to that of the earlier Greek intellectuals. Being consistent with the Greeks of the pre-Socratic period, Plato assumed ideal forms for material things and also for numbers and geometric forms. In addition to these forms Plato developed the view that ideal forms are related to values. For Plato, describing an object was never very far from valuing the object.[2] That is, when attempting to describe an object, likes and dislikes about the object are inevitably introduced. For example, whether a chair possesses the qualities of "chairness," or alternately, whether a chair is a smudged carbon copy of the "ideal chair," is directly related to how a chair is valued in terms of being either a "good" chair or a "poor" chair. Thus, the description of a chair as being either "big" or "small," "hard" or "soft," "pretty" or "ugly," or "expensive" or "cheap," all entail common elements about how a chair is valued. Although Plato had brought together three very important themes in philosophy, the last one, the application of ideal forms to value, was largely his own development.

Aristotle's Classical Realism. Aristotle, a student of the idealist Plato, stressed the inseparability of material and form. Aristotle believed that material objects, be they physical in nature, such as a chair, or intellectual in nature, such as an idea, were a distinct part of the world. To Aristotle, physical material always had form, although intellectual material, such as an idea, did not. Aristotle's metaphysics thus entailed both (1) his analysis of "being," for which he developed ten categories resulting from the way in which the verb "to be" can be used; and (2) his analysis of the problem of "becoming," that is, the causes for the existence of things. For Aristotle, reality essentially was teleological--purposive in essence. Thus Aristotle's description of reality was largely in contradiction to the views of Plato.[3]

Locke's Empiricism. By the thirteenth century, the efforts of Thomas Aquinas (1225-1274) and the Scholastics had largely refurbished the philosophical elements of earlier idealism with Aristotle's realism.[4] The efforts of Aquinas culminated in his great work, *Summa Theologica* (1267-73). Four centuries later the influence of idealism was further diminished by the work of John Locke (1632-1704), the middle-centuries English empiricist. Locke skeptically concluded that, "The world that we experience really does not exist, and the world that really does exist is not knowable."[5] In addition, the growing movement of natural philosophy (i.e., science) was strongly influencing the European intellectual community.

Kant's World of Noumenon and Phenomenon. It was largely through the efforts of such philosophers as Immanuel Kant (1724-1804) that a resurgence of philosophical idealism came about. To Kant, reality consisted of *noumenon*, rather than *phenomenon*.[6] Kant reasoned that it was only the *noumenal* world that was ultimately real, whereas the *phenomenal* world was limited to representing a determinism in the experiential world of space and time, one perhaps even scientifically exhaustible, but one not descriptive of ultimate reality. Kant's reasoning was motivated by his belief that man had an inherent need for moral freedom, a freedom that was becoming increasingly compromised by a view of the world grounded in the mechanistic determinism of science. For Kant, man's ability to freely make moral choices about right and wrong was of paramount importance.[7] To Kant, the *noumenal* world, in which things-in-themselves (i.e., *ding-an-sich*) existed, logically permitted individuals to maintain a freedom in their moral lives.[8]

Idealism/Realism and the University Tradition

Idealism and realism were the epistemological foundations for the scholarly disciplines that evolved within the academic structures of the early universities. Of the two, it is reasonable to conclude that idealism was dominant within American universities, at least until shortly after the Civil War. Partial evidence for this lies in the fact that the title "College of Arts and Letters" was commonly given to the primary academic units in pre-Civil

War universities. But during the last half of the nineteenth century science made major inroads into the academic structures of universities. It was during this period that the designation "Arts and Letters" in American universities increasingly was changed to the present day "Arts and Sciences."[9] Thus, at least the structural remnants of the two earlier divisions in human thought, idealism and realism, still exist in American universities. That is, idealism is reflected in the "arts" and realism is reflected in the "sciences."

There are other examples that present-day universities still highly value both idealism and realism as the primary structures of human thought. For example, traditionally the term "philosophy" in "Doctor of Philosophy" referred to a common root of knowledge; yet, the title "Doctor of Philosophy" is still used to signify the highest university degree. To a large extent this explains why academic doctorates are generally not designated "Doctor of Physics," "Doctor of English," "Doctor of History," or the like. Likewise, even the shift in the relative value of knowledge within the academic structures of many universities is indicative of the deep roots of both idealism and realism. This is perhaps most obvious in the designation of the core academic unit in many universities as the "*college* of arts and sciences." This designation literally means a body of philosophers having a common interest--in this case an interest in the intrinsic pursuit of knowledge.

Within colleges of arts and sciences broad academic divisions representing the humanities and the sciences eventually evolved. Within these two broad academic divisions second level academic "specializations" usually exist. Included among these are departments of history, languages, and music in the humanities, and physics, chemistry, and biology in the sciences. It is granted that the various departments within colleges of arts and sciences might have different views as to whether they have idealistic or realistic antecedents, or, for that matter, as to which division either should belong. But regardless of the association, the fundamental view that philosophy represents "love of knowledge" still prevails in colleges of arts and sciences. Such a regard for knowledge can rarely be justified solely by need and/or use; rather, it can predominantly be sustained through an intrinsic valuing of knowledge.

Although the intrinsic valuing of knowledge might itself be philosophically idealistic, realism also has developed an intrinsic valuing perspective in its own right. Regardless of the origins of the intrinsic pursuit of knowledge, today's realists do not generally view knowledge instrumentally. This is so perhaps for reasons different from those of the earlier realists. Thus, the fact that realists within the university also value knowledge intrinsically has further sharpened the dilemmas surrounding the functions of schools of education within the academic structures of universities.

Dilemmas of Valuing Knowledge in Schools of Education

The general function of schools of education within universities is in one sense instrumental. The nature of the instrumental dimension of the function of schools of education is grounded in the general societal expectation of public education, which is to pass on (teach) to the masses of society the knowledge of the liberal arts and sciences. Thus, the instrumentalism of schools of education is to complement the intrinsic nature of fundamental knowledge inherent in the arts and sciences. In order to fulfill their social expectations, schools of education would clearly have to collaborate with the broadly recognized "knowers" of the fundamental knowledge, the professors in the colleges of arts and sciences. If, on the other hand, schools of education attempted to educate the masses of society on the basis of the knowledge contained only within their own academic structures, then it would be highly questionable as to just what the nature of such knowledge would be. For instance, would schools of education be literally "universities" unto themselves, organizations with the wherewithal of both fundamental knowledge *and* the understanding of how to transmit that knowledge? If schools of education assumed such a stature, then they could easily disassociate themselves completely from universities and become independent educational institutions.

Thus, at first blush it might appear that the development of schools of education with universities was similar to those of other "professional" schools and colleges. This is not the case. The nature of the development of schools of education within academic structures of universities instead lies in the unique role that characterizes public education in the broader societal context. Because schools of education are colored by the general belief that they are in fact professional schools, the nature and function of "professional" schools within universities need to be explicated and then compared to those of schools of education.

5. The Professional Schools and Schools of Education

In universities, academic divisions outside of the traditional arts and sciences are most commonly viewed as "professional" schools or departments.

The first professional schools included those of medicine, law, and theology, which had their origins in the European universities.[10] Business administration, journalism, pharmacy, and engineering are more recent additions. In general, the academic programs of professional schools are considered to be either undergraduate or extensions of undergraduate degree programs. Often these programs are controlled within the specific professional school or department; however, in some universities, various professional programs are given graduate-degree status. In these instances the programs are usually part of a campus-wide graduate school. There are exceptions to this, namely where independent professional graduate schools exist within a university (e.g., a graduate school of business administration). Although in a distinct minority, there are also professional schools which are institutions completely separate from universities (e.g., independent colleges of pharmacy, law, or engineering) that might offer both undergraduate and graduate degrees. Many of these organizational and structural arrangements within which professional schools function have come about with the development of the many newer professional schools.

Newer Professional Schools

In American universities, the newer professional schools evolved from about 1820 to 1860, a period of great collegiate reform.[11] This was the time when the newer professions began to achieve greater status in the broader society. Just as today, the rise of some professional schools in universities, or as independent institutions of higher education, had been preceded by apprenticeship and propriety school training programs. Likewise, in order for the newer professions to increase their status in the broad society, they began to require some collegiate work as an entrance requirement. Thus it became increasingly necessary to make professional school degree programs at least appear to be as intellectually demanding as those in the arts and sciences. One strategy used by some professional schools to gain academic respectability was to require prospective students to successfully complete greater amounts of work in the arts and sciences prior to entering the professional school. Pharmacy is one of many examples of this. At the turn of the twentieth century, the usual entrance requirements into the profession of pharmacy was the completion of only grammar or elementary school.[12] By the 1950s the requirements increased to as much as a five-year college or university "professional" degree in pharmacy.[13] Since the turn of the century many other professional areas such as engineering, journalism, business administration, and nursing now require increasing lengths of academic preparation in higher education.

Ironically, the increased educational requirements for those seeking to enter a profession were frequently challenged by others already firmly established in those professions. For example, because of their lack of on-the-job training and experience, newly hired newspaper reporters graduating from schools of journalism often were viewed skeptically by their fellow employees. Needing a college degree as a prerequisite to be eligible for a position, yet having colleagues viewing job experience as being far more important, was a serious dilemma that confronted many of the newer professionals.

Theory and Practice in Professional Schools

Conflicts between the value and/or degree of theoretical and practical preparation for the professions had serious repercussions in the university.[14] The faculties of the arts and sciences had generally not been confronted by the necessity to justify by need and/or use what they professed. It was generally assumed that the knowledge of most worth existed within the academic structures of universities, and that this knowledge comprised the interests of the arts and sciences faculty. Likewise, the traditionalists believed that this body of knowledge was the product of many centuries of effort by scholars, just like those in present-day university colleges of arts and sciences, who were dedicated to seeking the "truth" through scholarly inquiry. *Ipso facto*, they believed that the only justification for inclusion of a particular "truth" in the academic structure of a university was the value it was given by the professors in the arts and sciences. Granted, how and why various fields of knowledge actually were included within the academic structures of universities differed greatly from the ideal beliefs of the traditionalists.

Archeology, for instance, is found today in some universities but not in most others. In universities where astronomy is part of the academic structure, it is often found in the physics department. In other universities, astronomy is a department in and of itself. Similar structural arrangements exist for other arts and sciences fields in universities; however, the structural arrangements within the arts and sciences tend to be stable over very long periods of time. This stability is due to the knowledge which these fields represent having withstood "the test of time."

But despite the long-standing tradition of according knowledge that has withstood the test of time a dominant place in the academic structures of universities, increasing pressures from the broad society eventually forced changes in these structures. It was the increasing value of instrumental knowledge in the broader society and the greater popularity and profusion of the newer professions that challenged the arts and sciences faculties for control of university academic structures. In this regard many of the growing number of first-generation university students expected something "practical" to ensue from many if not all of their courses.[15] Likewise, many aspiring electrical engineers who were required to take physics courses in "electricity and magnetism," for example, probably expected some practical application from even the theoretical dimensions of these courses.

When viewed from the perspective of the students, practical expectations from required courses for the engineering degree seemed reasonable. But, when viewed from the standpoint of the professor of physics, the demand for teaching the "practical applications" of theory undoubtedly seemed extraneous to the role of a university professor. Some professors of physics who found themselves in this situation might have pondered the question, "What scholarly justification can anyone have to request an acknowledged *knower* of physics to justify teaching about electricity and magnetism solely in terms of its usefulness?" Confronted with the idea that knowledge could be thought of solely for its instrumental value, the professor of physics was clearly faced with a dilemma not easily reconcilable. The professor might have reasoned that, because physics is simply inquiry about the fundamental truths of the physical universe, then the scholarly pursuit of physics need only be appreciated as basic knowledge--that is knowledge for its intrinsic worth.

Examples of the forgoing dilemma abound both historically and currently in American higher education. The idea of professors pursuing knowledge simply for its own sake has its origin and continues to persist within the liberal arts and sciences. But professors in professional schools, within traditional universities at least, also are expected to engage in the pursuit of knowledge. Yet, instrumental knowledge is so highly valued in the professions that the professional school professors who largely value knowledge intrinsically might be viewed by some professionals in the field as being ineffective. In fact, an overly strong intrinsic valuing of knowledge on the part of a professional school professor might even lead to the professor being viewed somewhat suspiciously by colleagues as being too much like the professors in the liberal arts and sciences. Likewise, administrative "sanctions" might be directed against such a "wayward" professional school professor. These peer and administrative responses would depend, of course, on both the academic stature of the faculty member in question and the extent to which the "applicability" of knowledge purportedly is being ignored.

An outgrowth of the conflict surrounding the value of just *what* is taught has further heightened differences not only between the traditional and newer professional schools but also between schools of education and colleges of arts and sciences. Analogous but substantially different issues exist within the arts and sciences. Included among these is the differences in beliefs about just what should to be considered "professional" knowledge. This conflict is compounded by many societal pressures being brought to bear on the arts and sciences faculties to make fundamental changes in the academic structures of their disciplines. Basically, these pressures are for greater professional orientation--however inconsistent this orientation is with the traditional ideal of the university professoriate. To a lesser degree, a similar but somewhat more subtle pressure is being exerted on the faculties of professional schools. This pressure is for these schools to be even more "practical" than they presently are.

Professional Orientation

Within universities the challenge for the professoriate to become more professionally oriented has manifested itself in many ways. Traditionally, tenure, promotion, and salary increases for university professors have depended on the individual professor's contributions to knowledge through research and creative effort, teaching, and service activities. Of these three activities, contributions to knowledge through research and creative efforts traditionally has far outweighed teaching and service. But, as universities have become more bureaucratic and highly rational organizations (in a logical positivistic sense of being "rational"), university administrators are attempting to replace value judgments with "facts" in such critical aspects of the university structure as the tenure and promotion process. The result is that the traditional criteria for tenure and promotion (and likewise those for salary increases) has been altered significantly, making the process more favorable for the professors in professional schools.

For example, in order to remove value judgments from salary decisions some administrators "quantify" research, teaching, and service activities by simply counting the number of published articles, classes and/or students taught, and papers read. In doing so, teaching and service functions are being given much more weight than they traditionally had been given. Yet, giving increased weight to these two activities, especially service, at the expense of research strongly favors the professional school professors. Over time, this practice has carried over into the decisions regarding tenure and promotion. Subsequently, this shift in emphasis has diminished research as the major function of the university professoriate as a whole.

Other factors, more in the political realm, have furthered epistemological and axiological controversies about knowledge between the arts and sciences, professional schools, and schools of education. These political factors are external but tangential to the academic structures of universities; nonetheless, they have helped to significantly change the power relationships between academic units in universities. For example, governing boards of universities now have many members who themselves have graduated with professional degrees. Being on governing boards places them in strategic positions to significantly influence the internal policies of universities that, in turn, change the power relationships between the professional schools, schools of education, and the arts and sciences. Also, the economic power of professional schools within universities has increased because many universities now are given large endowments to specifically promote particular professional fields of study.

Regardless of the depth of the conflict surrounding the intrinsic/ instrumental valuing of knowledge, it would hardly be in the best interest of either professional schools or schools of education to eliminate the role of the college of arts and sciences in their programs. It is the traditional arts and sciences, after all, that provide the fundamental knowledge base for the professional schools and, particularly, schools of education. Likewise, the knowledge that professors have about any particular field is highly valued by society as a whole, regardless of whether that knowledge is of an academic discipline in the traditional arts and sciences, a professional field, or the field of education. Yet, viewed in light of their primarily instrumental valuing of knowledge, it is questionable whether the academic nature of professional schools and schools of education can logically be considered to be consistent with the traditional university ideal of pursuing the truth wherever it might lead.

Knowledge and the Professional Schools

Simply stated, professional schools pick and choose from the arts and sciences that which they perceive to be important to their respective professions. They show little overt interest in the rest of the knowledge of the arts and sciences, with perhaps the exception of certain "core" courses required of all students in the university. Yet it is also apparent that professional schools and colleges of arts and sciences have different grounds for justifying their respective places in the university. In effect, the professional schools simply "want to know in order to be able to do," whereas the academic disciplines in the arts and sciences are concerned about "what it is they must do in order to know." Viewed in this light, the professional schools seek to offer that which they perceive as meeting the immediate needs of society.

But, is "meeting the needs of society" in and of itself sufficient grounds to justify a field of study being part of the academic structure of a university? In light of the traditional university ideal embodied in the liberal arts and sciences, the answer to this question is clearly "No." This is so because of the historical view of the liberal arts and sciences professoriate. That is, for a field of study to be considered scholarly it must first meet the fundamental and necessary condition that all knowledge within that field be constantly and forever open to critical inquiry. Logically this condition cannot hold if the only knowledge which is to count as being legitimate in a field is that knowledge bounded by the instrumental immediacy of societal needs. But the justification of knowledge by professional schools is, by its very nature, exclusively dependent on the immediacy of societal needs.

Knowledge and Schools of Education

Unlike professional schools, schools of education can be viewed in terms of two different instrumental perspectives. On the one hand, the knowledge-valuing function of professional schools is that of "picking and choosing" only that knowledge inherent in the academic disciplines of the arts and sciences which will advance their particular professions. On the other hand, the basic function of schools of education is to deliberately study how the knowledge of the arts and sciences can be transmitted.[16] In this regard, schools of education are full partners with the teachers in the public schools in their efforts to educate, as broadly as possible, the masses of society in the fundamental knowledge of humankind.

Because they are basically extensions of the arts and sciences, it would be inconsistent to view the public schools as essentially vocational in nature. Likewise, due to their emphasis on the "teaching" of a subject, many conclude that schools of education can value knowledge only instrumentally. But, since (1) the subjects that public school teachers teach are essentially comprised of the knowledge of the arts and sciences and (2) that the "teaching" of a subject cannot be disassociated from the subject itself, then schools of education are very much academically allied with colleges of arts and sciences, even in the intrinsic valuing of knowledge. This is rarely understood by the faculties of most universities, including those faculty members in schools of education. Such an understanding might be facilitated by first reviewing how society influences the valuing of knowledge within the academic structures of universities.

6. Societal Influence Upon the Valuing of Knowledge in the University

The role of the university in American society can be examined at several levels. At the broad societal level it can be contrasted to the role of the public schools. For example, in their most simplistic form, universities are institutions where persons ("scholars") who have been "normatively" recognized by other scholars to possess a great deal of knowledge about an academic field, "profess" this knowledge to students who "voluntarily" attend the institution for the purpose of acquiring this knowledge. And, in order to maintain their legitimacy, these "professors" of knowledge are expected to constantly seek new knowledge to add to their respective fields. On the other hand, public schools are governmentally mandated institutions where persons (teachers) who have been lawfully recognized through teacher licensing (i.e., certification) standards to have at least an acceptable minimum amount of knowledge about an academic field "teach" this knowledge to students who are, in turn, required by law to be in attendance. But, unlike university professors, public school teachers are not expected to advance their fields of knowledge in order to maintain their legitimacy. Likewise, it should be noted in this comparison that the knowledge which public school teachers teach is considered by the broader society to be of lesser scholarly worth than that taught by university professors.

Clearly, even a cursory analysis of the comparative functions of university professors and public school teachers reveals significant differences. Although important in their own right, the substantive differences between the functions of university professors and public school teachers is not at issue here. Rather, the issue here is the consequences of how these differences are perceived by those in the broader society.

The University as an Institution of "Knowers"

It is solely the professors and their knowledge that legitimate the traditional university ideal. This aspect of the academic structures of universities, that professors and their knowledge are fundamental to the very nature of universities, was developed centuries ago in the European universities and has prevailed in many research-based American universities from their very inception. The fact that professors were perceived as being extremely knowledgeable about a particular scholarly field probably was not in and of itself the entire reason for American society to highly value the institution of the university. After all, there also were many people outside of universities that were recognized for their knowledge. Included among these were independent scientists, well-known engineers and architects, famous artists, composers and actors, and even "captains of industry."

The beliefs about the American university professoriate that exist in the broader society are grounded in abstract values and, over time, have become institutionalized as "rational myths."[17] They are rational in that: (1) they have become associated with specific fundamentally important societal goals; (2) society has granted certain individuals or groups the exclusive right to determine the specific concomitant activities to achieve these goals and the qualifications of those members of society who want to help achieve these goals; and (3) these activities and qualifications have been specified in rule-like manner. These beliefs about the American university professoriate are myths because they are widely shared in the broader society.[18]

Many of the rational myths about universities become evident when examining the contradictions between (1) what society perceives to be of value about the knowledge that university professors are expected to have and (2) the actual conditions under which professors do their work. For example, professors who value knowledge intrinsically are not paid the higher salaries that many others in society are paid who are recognized for their instrumental knowledge. This likely has contributed to the prevailing myth that professors are as much or even more highly gratified by the process of advancing knowledge through inquiry than by the lure of higher salaries associated with endeavors that require largely instrumentally grounded knowledge. Despite their high levels of intelligence[19] and commitment to the pursuit of knowledge for its own sake, university professors are consider by many to be in a "fall-back" position. That is, they are professors simply because of some personal deficiency that prevents them from using their knowledge for monetary gain. This is evidenced by the well-known cliché in the medical profession, "those who can, practice; those who can't, teach." But the significance and importance of the historic dedication of the university professoriate to the intrinsic pursuit of knowledge can not be readily dismissed simply because valuing knowledge intrinsically is presently "unpopular" in the broader society. For example, the general societal perception of just what kind of knowledge (intrinsic or instrumental) university professors can value while still fulfilling a legitimate societal role can have a major influence on the developing academic structure of the modern American university. Presently, for example, the high value placed on instrumental knowledge in the broader society is directly reflected in the organizational structure that is the foundation of the American economic system, namely the business corporation. Because of the pervasive nature of the economic system, the business/corporate organizational structure has, over time, become institutionalized as the most "rational" structure for virtually all organizations, including universities.

Universities and Business Corporations: Conflicting Roles and Expectations

There are strong indications today that many American business corporations have made significant inroads into the traditional academic domain of universities. High levels of expenditures for educational and training programs for employees have been reported by many large corporations.[20] Business/corporate education and training programs range from very brief job acquaintance sessions through programs lasting several days, weeks, or even months. Often business corporations make funds available so that their employees can enroll, often on company time, in educational/training programs at local colleges, universities, and other institutions. At still other times, corporations contract for education and training services with specialized education/training business corporations or individuals who are considered to be experts in their respective fields but are not associated with any institution of higher education. And, in some cases, business corporations conduct their own academic degree programs, some of which are even sanctioned by regional educational accreditation agencies controlled by colleges and universities. It can be logically assumed that business corporations which provide educational and training programs for their employees do so with expectations of a return on their investment in such programs. Because of the profit-motive "bottom line" mentality of most American corporations, it would be rare indeed for a corporation to justify an educational expenditure solely for an employee's personal intrinsic satisfaction.

But as organizations, the most fundamental distinction between legitimate universities and business corporations is the profit motive.[21] Clearly, business corporations in the American capitalistic economy exist only if they make a profit; therefore, business corporations that are more concerned about the welfare of their employees than making a profit for their shareholders will simply fail to survive for very long. On the other hand, unlike successful business corporations, legitimate universities make no claim that they exist to make a monetary gain. When a university does exist solely to do so, then society imposes at least informal sanctions, like dubbing it with the ignominious distinction of being a "diploma mill." But if (1) society does not expect the structure and functions of legitimate universities to be like those of business corporations, yet (2) business corporations can legitimately provide educational services, then (3) what accounts for society's expectation that universities should increasingly transmit knowledge that is immediately useful and beneficial to business corporations? This is a particularly important question because the transmission of useful (instrumental) knowledge is done both at great financial burden to society and at the expense of the historic university role of pursuing knowledge intrinsically.

Contradictions in the Role of the Professor

The proliferation of organizations generally--particularly large business/corporate organizations--within modern societies is substantial evidence that society is increasingly adopting an "organization culture." Because university professors live in the broader society, they too, like most others, likely adopt the culture of the society, including beliefs about how organizations should be structured and how they should function. But, when dealing with the university as an organization that is distinctly different--in the traditional and historically ideal sense--from business and corporate organizations, university professors are faced with fundamental contradictions. These contradictions are a result of the way society perceives (1) the roles of actors within organizations generally and (2) the roles of professors within universities as unique organizations. The contradictions are brought more sharply into focus when two important facts are considered. First, the university as a formal organization developed centuries before the modern business corporation came into existence. Second, professors in modern universities have lived exclusively in an "organization culture," a culture in which the archetypal organization is the ubiquitous business corporation.

Being part of a broader society where a particular organizational rationality is now a significant aspect of its culture, university professors must struggle with the contradiction of being expected to function in a role seemingly inconsistent with the prevailing rationality. This role has significant historical antecedents which are still part of the culture of the university, if not the broader society. Thus, contradictions arise when the role of the professor is examined in terms of (1) its consistency with that of the historic university ideal, (2) the fact that this ideal is clearly not of a profit-making orientation, and (3) the need of the professor to concurrently function in a broader society with its business corporation organizational rationality. As this rational myth about organizations becomes even more deeply ingrained in the American culture, a clarification of the contradictions surrounding the role of university professors becomes crucial to gaining a clearer understanding of the modern American university.

It was pointed out earlier that American universities include at least a college of arts and sciences, usually professional schools, and often a school of education as distinct academic entities. It also was argued that professional schools value knowledge more instrumentally than do colleges of arts and sciences or schools of education. In this regard, the professional schools simply "pick and choose" from the knowledge of specific academic fields of study which the arts and sciences have intrinsically pursued. If these aspects are truly descriptive of the academic structure of universities, then some mediating factor must be present within the university itself which has prompted society to believe that the organizational structure of a university should be more bureaucratic, like that of a business enterprise in the corporate world, than collegial, like that of the historical university ideal.

Organizational Structure and the University

There is indeed considerable evidence that the university has become more responsive to the general societal belief that virtually all legitimate organizations should function like business/corporate enterprises. For example, the university has developed massive hierarchal bureaucratic administrative structures where once there were relatively flat collegial structures for governance and administration.[22] More importantly, in order to maintain social legitimacy the university has created new academic entities and modified some already existing ones. This is evident in the proliferation of professional schools that provide a reservoir of potential employees "educated" in the instrumental (*qua* technical) knowledge needed to support the business/corporate world. If this connection between professional schools in universities and personnel-hiring practices in the business/corporate world were non-existent, then what other factors would justify the presence of so many technically based professional schools within the university?

Schools of business, for example, justify their existence within the academic structures of universities on the quality of the pertinent instrumental knowledge that they can pass on to their graduates. With such knowledge, it is assumed that these graduates can more effectively manage business/corporate organizations in the broader society. On the other hand, if schools of business would justify their existence on the grounds that they fundamentally value knowledge intrinsically, then many alternative questions could be raised. Most obvious among these would be: Why did business, as a field of knowledge, not evolve centuries ago in a manner parallel to mathematics, science, history, and the like? But, clearly, the history of the university shows that schools of business did not develop within the academic structures of universities for the same reasons that the more traditional academic fields did.

Because schools of business are preoccupied with valuing knowledge instrumentally, rather than valuing knowledge intrinsically like the more traditional academic fields, then important questions also can be raised about just how schools of business maintain their legitimacy within the academic structures of universities. Included among these questions, and most important for this discussion, would be: (1) How did the field of business become established in the academic structures of universities, whereas countless other areas of endeavor have not? and (2) What accounts for schools of business having an increasing share of the undergraduate degrees in many universities today? The answer to these questions must lie in the expectations --and their antecedent values--that exist in the societal environment within which the modern university exists.[23]

Parallel questions can also be raised in regard to other fields which primarily value knowledge instrumentally yet are within the academic structures of universities--but almost always outside of colleges of arts and sciences. Because knowledge was almost exclusively valued intrinsically in traditional universities, then, like schools of business, most academic units that value knowledge instrumentally--most notably the newer professional schools --were also instituted within the academic structures of universities by forces inherent in the broad societal environment. Upon closer examination, there is considerable evidence that these social forces are conditioned by the business/corporate organization mentality that has proliferated within almost every aspect of modern American society. If these social forces are powerful enough to significantly alter the academic structures of traditional universities--and in turn the fundamental valuing of knowledge orientation of universities--then their power to alter other structures of the university needs to be examined.

Profit Making and the University Ideal

It is at the micro-level that the differences between the roles of professional schools, schools of education, and colleges of arts and sciences within universities are seen to be analogous to those existing at the macro-level between the unique roles of the university and of business/corporate organizations in the broader society. For example, if professional schools have a strong predilection to "pick and choose" from basic knowledge only that which they find useful, then it would be inconsistent for professional school professors within university academic communities *not* to value--at least to some marginal psychologically acceptable degree--the "bottom line" profit-motive ideology of the business/corporate world. But any ideology enduring for very long in the environment of the university--an environment which ideally conceived essentially eschews the narrow sense of rationality inherent in every ideology--is a logical contradiction. Yet this contradiction exists within the modern American university. It does so largely without being widely recognized by many in the broader society. The fact that the university has historically provided an essentially intrinsic knowledge-valuing environment for all academic units, including the professional schools, simply compounds the contradiction. This contradiction is further sharpened because legitimate universities make no claim to have profit-making ends as an essential aspect of their fundamental nature. Yet, many legitimate universities do tolerate and even strongly encourage their faculty members to engage in such quasi profit-making endeavors as "professional" consulting and community "service" activities.

It is common knowledge in many universities that some faculty members of professional schools derive significantly more income from their professional consulting activities than they do from their university salaries. But consulting activities can make inordinate demands on the time of faculty members, thus encroaching on both the quantity and quality of their teaching and research activities. Nevertheless, many universities strongly encourage their faculty members to engage in consulting activities with industry, business, and the government because the university believes that it will enhance their public "image." Thus, the members of the faculty, especially professional school professors, are apt to be seen by some university governing boards and administrators as "public relations" resources.

Another more modern function of the university professoriate is community service. This function is often very broadly defined and can include a wide range of activities. But community service activities also can demand an inordinate amount of time and create a variety of work-related stresses which, in turn, affect the overall performance of a university professor. Although monetary compensation might be derived, it is not necessarily the primary factor that motivates universities to encourage their faculties to engage in community service functions. Universities, like many other service institutions, exist in social environments where resources are allocated through dynamic and often complex political processes. Because public resources are limited and the competition for them is often very keen, university governing boards and administrators perceive the need to significantly enhance the legitimacy of their institutions by improving their public image. Thus, the motive exists for linking community service activities to faculty salaries.

In a parallel manner, a faculty member might also expend considerable time rendering service within the university itself. This usually takes the form of a variety of committee (or the more modern "task force") activities ranging from the level of the academic department to that of the governing board. Because faculty committees still exist even though the university has been almost thoroughly bureaucratized, the motive for retaining the faculty committee system is questionable. One logical explanation is that in order to reinforce the legitimacy of universities their governing boards and administrators want the public to believe that modern universities, in the tradition of the great universities of the past, are still being administered and governed collegially.[24]

In light of the basic societal beliefs about the role of the university professors as knowledge seekers, serious ethical questions arise when universities overemphasize the professional consulting and community service functions of the modern professoriate. In the ideal sense of the university tradition, the remuneration for professional consulting and community service activities that are rendered by university professors should, at best, be a very minor factor in legitimating the role of the professoriate. But, rendering service without just compensation would be a contradiction for university professors who, after all, are also members of the broader society where receiving compensation for virtually all work has acquired the status of a right. Clearly, the difference between professional consulting and community service activities being performed with or without compensation is at the heart of the contradictions surrounding the intrinsic/instrumental valuing of knowledge controversy within the context of the traditional university ideal.

The Intrinsic Valuing of Knowledge and the Modern American University

The demands by the professions and the business world for a pool of trained personnel sufficiently demonstrates that they highly value instrumental knowledge. That society not only tolerates these demands but also devotes significant resources to meet them, likewise is evidence of how highly society itself values instrumental knowledge. But what is more important for the discussion here is that society demands that this passing on (teaching) of instrumental knowledge should take place within the academic structures of universities. Because the intrinsic value of knowledge is deeply imbedded within their organizational cultures, the transmission of instrumental knowledge as a major, if not primary, function of modern universities has brought about major fundamental contradictions within their structures.

On the one hand, the pursuit of knowledge for its own sake by the traditional university professoriate clearly betrays a basic intrinsic valuing of knowledge. It is the intrinsic valuing of knowledge that makes the university more consistent with its historic role in society, namely, the open and unrestricted pursuit of the truth, wherever it might lead. Unlike business enterprises, universities make contributions to the commonweal of society regardless of any monetary rewards or "profits." Continued misrepresentation of the valuing of knowledge within the universities can therefore lead to the universities being suspected of having profit motives inherent within the professoriate, thus making society suspect of the particular "truth" being revealed. At worst, the university, instead of being a neutral institution in the social fabric, could be perceived as being a willing partner with the business/corporate world in seeking higher and higher profits, perhaps even at the expense of other institutions and individuals in society. It is this fundamental difference in the valuing of knowledge--intrinsic versus instrumental--that lends legitimacy to the view that the intrinsic pursuit of knowledge, with its potential for revealing infinite rationalities, should prevail in the American university. On the other hand, care must be taken not to discount the societal benefits derived from the instrumental valuing of knowledge within the traditional academic structures of universities. The application of knowledge generated within a university indeed can be of value to both the university and the broader society which it serves; nevertheless, the limited rationality inherent in the instrumental valuing of knowledge should preclude it from having a dominant role in the academic structures of universities. After all, the origins and future preservation of the university ideals of *Lehrfreiheit* and *Lernfreiheit*--freedom to teach and freedom to learn--depends on the intrinsic valuing of knowledge inherent in the liberal arts and sciences. This presents significant problems for the modern American university.[25] If the American university and its societal relationships with the professions and the business/corporate world are to retain the essential aspects of the historic university ideal, then a symbiotic relationship between the liberal arts and sciences, the professional schools, and schools of education must be both encouraged and nurtured.

NOTES

1. These myths persist despite studies to the contrary. For example, in about 1948 Goddard made a comparison of secondary education majors as a group to all other students taking the same botany courses in the previous ten years at the University of Pennsylvania. He reported that, "...the average scores of the students in secondary education were just as good as the average scores of college students generally, whether men or women." See David A. Goddard, "The College of Education Within the University," in *The Role of the College of Education Within the University*, ed. Anthony Scarangello (Newark, Delaware: University of Delaware, 1969), p. 52. In a similar study in 1982, Stolee found that, "The mean average of the education majors was above that of the non-education majors in subject matter courses *within the academic majors of the non-education majors* (emphasis added)." See Michael J. Stolee, *Quality of School of Education Students and Graduates* (Milwaukee: University of Wisconsin-Milwaukee, 1982), pp. 1-3, cited in Charles W. Case and William A. Matthews, *Colleges of Education: Prospectives on their Future* (Berkeley, California: McCutchan, 1985), p.10.

2. On this topic Brumbaugh and Lawrence noted that, "...it was Plato's contribution to recognize that ideals, goals, and criteria are ends to which form, in the sense of definite structure, is a means, and that ideals actually operate as causes in nature and human life. Plato saw that neither evaluating something or describing it can be carried very far without the other. As a result he refused to separate questions of *fact* from those of *value*." See Robert S. Brumbaugh and Nathaniel M. Lawrence, *Philosophers on Education:*

Six Essays on the Foundations of Western Thought (Boston: Houghton Mifflin, 1963), p. 13.

3. As noted by Burns and Brauner, "Plato's most famous student, Aristotle (384-322), did not agree with Platonic metaphysics, nor did he agree with Democratus and other atomists; consequently, in developing his own metaphysics he followed the rule of the golden mean by mediating the Materialism of the pre-Socratic and the Idealism of the Socratics." See Hobert W. Burns and Charles J. Brauner, *Philosophy of Education: Essays and Commentaries* (New York: The Ronald Press, 1962), p. 95.

4. This became known as *Thomistic dualism*, ". . . a blend of early Greek Materialism and later Greek Idealism; it is a blend of the Idealistic Plato and the Realistic Aristotle, with the heavier dosage being Aristotelian . . ." See Burns and Brauner, p. 97.

5. George Berkeley (1685-1753), the famous Irish bishop, gave a renewed emphasis to idealism after the skepticism of John Locke had weakened its status. Burns and Brauner, p. 79.

6. Georg Hegel (1770-1831), an idealistic philosopher, charged that because Kant divided reality into *noumenon* and *phenomenon*, then Kantian idealism was simply a dualism. Since the real world that Kant had postulated was the world of *noumenon* (i.e., *ding-an-sich*), Hegel's charge of Kant being a dualist is generally disregarded. Furthermore, Hegel stripped Kant's *noumenal* world of any kind of existence. He argued that Kant's "thing" in itself was an abstraction. For a more detailed discussion of Hegel's view of Kant's *noumenon*, see Burns and Brauner, p. 83.

7. The important thing that one needs to understand about Immanuel Kant's world is that it is, "...a deterministic world to the extent that it is merely an object of knowledge. But to the extent that the world is an arena of action, the agency of moral action may be in the rational self and may therefore be free, i.e., self-determined (not undetermined). The real contrast is between an acting self which is other-determined and one which is self-determined." See Brumbaugh and Lawrence, p. 100.

8. For a particularly interesting discussion of an interpretation of the Kantian moral ethic and the conception of justice, see John Rawls, *A Theory of Justice* (Cambridge, Massachusetts: Harvard University Press, 1971), pp. 251-57.

9. For a more complete discussion of the change in title from "college of arts and letters" to "college of arts and sciences" and the like, see Henry R. Weinstock, "An Analysis of Issues in Liberal and Professional Undergraduate Education" (Ed.D. diss., University of Georgia, 1965).

10. The traditional professions of law, medicine, and theology were followed by many other fields claiming to be professions. For a further elaboration, see Weinstock, p. 56.

11. See George L. Newsome, Jr., "American University Patterns, 1776-1900: A Study of Six Selected Universities" (Ph.D. diss., Yale University, 1956), p. 152.

12. For a complete discussion of the history of pharmacy in higher education, see Lloyd E. Blauch, "The Pharmaceutical Curriculum," *Higher Education* 9 (October 1953): 26.

13. Blauch, p. 25.

14. In this regard it can be said that, "Granting that certain kinds of knowledge and skills are required in vocational callings, such knowledge or skills are not necessarily professional or scholarly enough to merit a place in university education. Perhaps this sort of reasoning led university officials of the nineteenth century to exclude most of the professions from universities." See Weinstock, p. 69.

15. The increasing demand for "practical" or vocational types of education at the university level is still taking place today. But Bowen and Schuster believe that the demand might be leveling off because of five fundamental changes that are occurring in the broader society. These changes are: 1. The womens' movement; 2. Larger numbers of second-generation college students who, in the past, have usually opted for a more liberal education than what their parents had pursued; 3. The new age of "high technology," which will reduce the need for greater numbers of technically educated students; 4. The overcrowding of many of the professions such as law, medicine, and dentistry; and 5. Signs that there are concerns in the broader society of the negative consequence of a constantly growing number of technically educated professionals. See Howard R. Bowen and Jack H. Schuster, *American Professors* (New York: Oxford University Press, 1986), pp. 125-26.

16. It has been pointed out that, "...members of a school of education faculty are concerned with an instrumental understanding of just *how* the fundamental knowledge contained in the intrinsically-valued arts and sciences is transmitted. Hence, the research function of an education faculty thus largely takes the role of systematically enhancing a body of knowledge about such a transmitting process. When viewed in this sense, therefore, a school of education faculty is evidently not a repository of fundamental human knowledge; rather, it is an aid in getting as much of this fundamental knowledge to as many people as possible." See Henry R. Weinstock, "Comparing a School of Education to the College of Arts and Sciences and

Professional Schools in a University," *Proceedings of the Southwestern Philosophy of Education Society* 33 (1983): 161.

17. For a discussion of the concept of "rational myths," see John W. Meyer and W. Richard Scott, *Organizational Environments: Ritual and Rationality* (Beverly Hills, California: Sage Publications, 1983), p. 14.

18. The best explanation of just what a myth is as used here was given by Mark Shorer in his book *William Blake*. Shorer noted that a myth is, "...a *large, controlling image* founded in man's experience (not a concept abstracted and detached from all sensible referents); not false by definition, it might be *true* as it can be; it is not anti-intellectual, not *the negative or the contrary* of ideas, but their basis and their structure; mystic images are the elements, however submerged, by which thought is *sustained* and propelled, and by means of which ideas--those systems of abstractions, for example, that we call ideologies--activate behavior; our own civilization *seems to be struggling toward a myth that will be explicitly ethical, even political.*" See Mark Shorer, *William Blake* (New York: Henry Holt & Company, 1946), cited in Henry A. Murray, "Introduction," *Daedalus* 88 (Spring 1959): 212-13. For this quotation and a further discussion of the implication of myth for educational policy, see Charles J. Fazzaro, "Myth, Metaphor and Educational Policy," *Proceedings of the Southwestern Philosophy of Education Society* 34 (1984): 1-9.

19. For a contemporary discussion of the intelligence of professors, see Bowen and Schuster, p. 25.

20. A company that attempts to keep a listing of the various types and number of "seminars" for business and industry, 1st Seminar Service, listed over 100,000 being offered in 1987. They estimated that over 8 million people are trained a year at a cost to business and industry of about $4 billion. See Richard Conniff, "In Chicago: Seminars Everywhere," *Time* (12 October 1987): 12.

21. For a more complete discussion of the differences between a university and a business enterprise, see Charles J. Fazzaro, "The University as a Business, or Are Students Like Corvettes," *National Forum* 66 (Spring 1986): 32-34.

22. See Fazzaro, "The University as a Business, or Are Students Like Corvettes."

23. In 1939, Clarence Marsh published an excellent history of business administration in higher education. In commenting on the first school of business he pointed out that the concept of education in the new professions, as contrasted to the grand old triad of law, medicine, and theology, was put into practice one hundred twenty-five years ago, (1835), the first collegiate

school of business not being established until 1881. This was at the University of Pennsylvania, being founded as the Wharton School of Finance and Commerce. See Clarence S. Marsh, "Business Education at the College Level," *American Council on Education Studies* 3, no. 7 (March 1939): 8.

24. Whether modern American universities are governed collegially, or bureaucratically like business organizations, also has implications for the valuing of knowledge, but this issue is too complicated to be fully addressed here.

25. The concepts of *Lehrfreiheit* and *Lernfreiheit* were the foundation of academic freedom in German universities. They originated and gained significance in the University of Halle in the early 1700s. See Kern Alexander and Edwin Solomon, *College and University Law* (Charlottesville, Virginia: Michie, 1972), p. 343, cited by Charles J. Fazzaro, "Four Myths of the American University and Their Influences on Its Development," *Social Science* (Summer 1976): 139-48. More than merely allowing professors to teach and students to learn without fear, true academic freedom is an atmosphere within which the entire academic endeavors of a university is to take place. For a complete history and discussion of academic freedom in the United States, see Richard Hofstadler and Walter Metzger, *The Development of Academic Freedom in the United States* (New York: Columbia University Press, 1955).

Three

The Valuing of Knowledge
Transformed

Overview

The explosion of knowledge during the Enlightenment of seventeenth-
and eighteenth-century Europe was fueled by a broad reawakening to the
personal and societal benefits of human inquiry. Growing numbers of scholars
in the expanding universities of the period were inquiring about the meaning
and explanation of virtually everything that could be thought about and/or
experienced. This pivotal period of Western history also spawned the widespread belief in *jus naturale*, natural law. These fundamental contributions to
Western society, the explosion of knowledge and its grounding in both the
personal and social benefits of human inquiry and natural law, are particularly
significant for the more recent transformation in the valuing of knowledge.
They are in every sense the foundations of the contradictions that have arisen
between the principles of American democracy and a system of public
education that has become grounded in an instrumental valuing of knowledge.
Significant in the development of these contradictions between the fundamental principles of American democracy and public education is the role of
the university.

The explosion of knowledge and the political liberalism precipitated
by the Enlightenment contributed to institutionalizing within the structures of
Western universities the previously cited concepts of *Lehrfreiheit* and
Lernfreiheit, freedom to teach and learn. With the freedom to pursue
practically any knowledge, university professors could now justify valuing

knowledge intrinsically, for its own sake. But it was not until the late nineteenth century that modern universities had to contend with serious conflicts between (1) the intrinsic valuing of knowledge that, over centuries, became institutionalized within their academic structures and (2) the instrumental valuing of knowledge that was rapidly growing in importance in the broader society. It was societal pressures to include more professional schools within their academic structures that in turn forced universities to acclimate within their faculties increasing numbers of professors who valued knowledge instrumentally.

But more importantly for the American democracy, the Enlightenment fostered a new view of the relationship between people and the state. Ideas of the most notable moral philosophers of the Enlightenment became the basis for modern liberal democratic and egalitarian principles. Particular among the luminaries of that era were Thomas Hobbes (1588-1679), John Locke (1632-1704), David Hume (1711-1776), Jean Jacques Rousseau (1712-1778), and Immanuel Kant (1724-1804). Although their views on human nature and the interrelationship of people in social systems differed in many ways, these intellectual giants generally considered the state to be a legitimate instrument of human progress. Likewise, they generally agreed, again in their own distinctive ways, that the ideal role of the state as an instrument of human progress could not occur unless the state clearly recognized that each individual possessed an inherent set of human rights, and concomitant civil liberties, which precluded the imposition of repressive constraints by the state.

Consequently, with the institutionalizing of both academic freedom within the universities and civil liberties within the broader society, conditions existed for the development of significant contradictions between American democratic ideals and the instrumental valuing of knowledge that predominates today in American public education. What was needed to finally create these contradictions was a bridge to connect modern liberal democratic principles to the valuing of knowledge. That bridge was the incorporation of the principles of free speech in the First Amendment of the Constitution.

Since the ideal state of free speech, which includes thought and expression,[1] requires that there be no official orthodoxy, then government must not only recognize but also tolerate the possibility, at least, of the existence of an infinite number of rationalities. On the other hand, the discovered "truths" of realism, manifested through the instrumental valuing of knowledge, implies a limited rationality. Even the possibility of a limited rationality--a world existing independent of the mind--opens the door for orthodoxies to be institutionalized *de facto*, through incremental institutional and/or governmental policies, or *de jure*, through overt legislative acts and judicial decisions. In American higher education the transformation from an intrinsic to an instrumental valuing of knowledge has evolved through both *de facto* and *de jure* means. For example, as a response to societal pressures to accommodate more professional schools universities subsequently moved more to valuing knowledge instrumentally. Compounding the pressure to accommodate more professional schools, state-supported universities were almost simultaneously pressured, by the imposition of licensing standards for public school teachers, to provide academic programs to prepare teachers for the public schools.

Of course these changes in the fundamental academic structure of American universities were not sudden. They occurred over the better part of the nineteenth and twentieth centuries and involved the development of new institutions within higher education. The most significant of these was the "junior" college. In the evolution of higher education in the United States the junior/community college is an institution that has played a significant role in shaping the valuing of knowledge in the broader society. Initially, the junior college provided the first two years of a four-year college or university education for students who did not attend a baccalaureate degree-granting institution. Because of their easy accessibility, lack of an institutionalized value for the importance of research, and declining enrollments,the junior colleges found it relatively easy to transform their academic structures from an emphasis on the liberal arts to an emphasis on practical or vocational programs.

The first "practical" programs that junior colleges offered were pre-professional. These programs were adopted to accommodate the growing number of students wanting to obtain a degree from the new professional schools then developing in universities. One consequence of this shift in academic program emphasis was a fundamental change in the educational character of junior college faculties. During the change the faculties included increasing numbers of not only university-prepared graduates but also skilled craftsmen and practitioners who taught vocational-type courses. Thus, changes in the fundamental nature of their faculties brought about the development of contradictions in how the junior colleges fundamentally value knowledge in light of both the nature of their origin and society's perception of their intended function. Likewise, changes in the fundamental academic structure of junior colleges brought about significant contradictions between their new character and their higher-education heritage.

These contradictions were conspicuous since the junior colleges continued to use the traditional academic labels, such as title of "professor," a designation which has great historical import for the university. Before the transformation of the junior colleges and the development of professional schools within universities, a "professor" was viewed as a person who valued knowledge intrinsically. After the transformation, the title also came to include those persons whose practical and applied interests clearly demonstrated that they valued knowledge instrumentally, not intrinsically. While universities struggled to resolve the contradictions between the arts and sciences tradition of valuing knowledge intrinsically and the new professional schools penchant for valuing knowledge instrumentally, they also had to struggle with these very same contradictions in regard to the education of prospective public school teachers. Although these contradictions surrounding the valuing of knowledge were fundamentally the same, they arose from significantly different origins.

For instance, in order to adequately prepare public school teachers the university had to first determine just which university experiences would be appropriate in light of the university intrinsic/ideal and the societal instrumental/real. This problem was further compounded by the society's significantly different perceptions about the purposes of elementary schools and high schools. Because society expected high school students to know about things (e.g., history and literature), prospective high school teachers were therefore expected to be very knowledgeable in at least one academic area. In order to meet these societal expectations, the university required prospective high school teachers to complete a major or at least the near-equivalent of a major in one of the arts and sciences. Subsequently, because their primary role models were liberal arts and sciences professors, who derive their value of knowledge through scholarly inquiry, prospective high school teachers were likely to also have developed a predilection to value knowledge intrinsically.

On the other hand, society generally expected elementary schools to teach students the "basics" of education (e.g., how to read and write). To meet these societal expectations the elementary education programs within the university therefore required prospective elementary teachers to know more about *how* to teach rather than to have a comprehensive knowledge of the subjects to be taught. Because most prospective elementary teachers took only the first two years of their work in the arts and sciences, they had less academic exposure to professors who value knowledge intrinsically. On the other hand, because prospective elementary teachers were significantly more involved with education professors who were largely concerned about how teachers should teach, then elementary teachers were more inclined to acquire an instrumental value of knowledge.

From this history it is evident that prospective public school teachers who study in a university are faced with the same fundamental contradictions inherent in the intrinsic/instrumental knowledge-valuing conflict that exists between the arts and sciences and schools of education. But the contradictions in the valuing of knowledge are more perplexing for prospective elementary teachers than they are for high school teachers. This is so because high school teachers are usually required to complete at least a near major in one of the liberal arts and sciences. In so doing, they are more apt to acquire a value of knowledge more consistent with that of the traditional university ideal.

This difference in preparation programs is consistent with the beliefs in the broader society about what both high school teacher preparation and elementary teacher preparation programs should foster. Evidence that society does in fact believe that high school and elementary teachers should be prepared differently can be found in the vast differences between high school and elementary teacher licensing standards. Most states in fact require high school teachers to have at least a near major in at least one or more academic fields; whereas, elementary teachers are more often required to have significant preparation in methods of teaching, child development, and the like. These differences, in turn, are clearly reflected in the perceptions that elementary education professors have about knowledge and their resulting attitudes towards such knowledge.

Lastly, the clash between the valuing of knowledge in university-based preparation programs for high school and elementary teachers has heightened the severity of the contradictions which junior high/middle school students must face. For schools of education within the academic structures of universities, this also has led to many problems both (1) between the arts and sciences professors and professors of education and (2) among high school and elementary school professors within the schools of education themselves.

7. The University Influence on the Junior/Community College

A variety of institutions have emerged within the evolving structure of American higher education. Among these are the traditional universities, state universities, teachers colleges, junior/community colleges, normal schools, technical institutes, and independent professional schools and colleges. At its inception, at least, it was the junior college that served as a link between the high school and the university. For this reason the junior college was for some of those who wanted a collegiate education the most important academic institution that had emerged during the late 1800s and the early 1900s.[2] Although junior colleges, as they were first conceived, are rather rare today, their contemporary educational structures are more popularly known as "community" colleges.[3] Notwithstanding that the different names that this institution has adopted in its transformation might be significant in themselves, the focus of the clarification here is on the contradictions arising from the valuing of knowledge within these institutions and the structural characteristics they have borrowed from the university.

The Junior College Student

In the early part of the twentieth century those who wanted a college or university degree had to attend four-year institutions. More often than not, these institutions were located a great distance from where most prospective students lived. In the Midwest and Far West smaller and more readily accessible "junior" colleges soon developed.[4] In California many junior colleges were actually extensions of the high school and even shared the same buildings.[5] In New England the junior colleges evolved from the private academies that could no longer compete with the rapidly growing number of public high schools.[6] In the Middle Atlantic states many junior colleges evolved from normal schools. These two-year institutions rapidly became a suitable alternative for many young people to begin their higher education. Thus, in its initial stage of development the junior college became an institution where many prospective college students could complete their first two years of a four-year college program.[7]

Although the students who attended junior colleges were from a variety of cultures and socioeconomic backgrounds, they were similar in at least family obligations and resources of time.[8] Why they did not attend four-year colleges or universities away from home can likely be explained by both factors that disguise deeply seated personal reasons and other factors which were imposed on them by the broader culture. For instance, some students probably viewed their rural backgrounds as having rendered them to be socially and culturally inferior. For others, their sex or being a member of a racial minority militated against their attending major colleges and universities, regardless of where these institutions were located. And for still others, there were *de jure* and *de facto* societal restrictions based on religious and ethnic factors.

Likewise, in the early part of the twentieth century, at least, there were social norms and parental fears that prevented many women from attending any institution of higher education.[9] In still other instances, the academic rigor of some colleges and universities made many students hesitant about attending any four-year institution of higher education. Regardless of the reasons that many prospective college students of that time had for attending junior colleges, the point here is that they all wanted to acquire an education beyond the high school. What is more, they wanted that education to be similar in academic status (i.e., earning an academic degree) to the education they could have acquired at a four-year college or university.

The Junior College Curriculum

To a large extent, the academic programs in the early junior colleges mirrored the first two years of the general academic programs of most four-year baccalaureate degree-granting institutions.[10] Consequently, the junior college became an increasingly acceptable option for those who aspired to eventually attend a four-year college or university, and many students took advantage of this opportunity.[11] But over the years pressures from the broader society forced junior colleges to drastically change their academic programs. For instance, when unemployment was high, such as it was during the great depression of the 1930s and succeeding economic recessions, the junior colleges also prepared people for "gainful employment" (i.e., provided vocational training) as well as preparing some for four-year colleges and universities.[12] The nature of these programs, intended to prepare people for jobs, further technical training, or a technically orientated education at a university, were reflected in changes in parallel professional school programs in universities. For example, university engineering programs soon began, in turn, to reflect related technological and pre-engineering programs in junior colleges.

It was also about this time that similar professional school-type programs rapidly emerged at the junior college level under the rubric of "pre-professional" programs. It was in this regard that some junior college course-work began to take on a decided vocational character. On the other hand, these newer programs also reflected the nature of the newer "professional" programs that were likewise being developed within the liberal arts colleges of many universities. Included among these programs were journalism, business administration, and home economics. As history has shown, many of these "professional" programs within liberal arts colleges eventually became independent professional schools unencumbered by the restraints of the liberal arts faculties.[13] Nonetheless, many junior colleges soon began to claim that their pre-professional programs were equivalent to the first two years of a four-year college program. Partly because of this claim pre-professional courses and programs rapidly became prominent in junior colleges.

Because of the wide diversity of programs that junior colleges were now offering, anomalies began to emerge between the academic structures of the junior college and the traditional four-year baccalaureate degree institutions. In addition, for the junior colleges to adequately staff the wide spectrum of courses that they were now offering--from the pure liberal arts to the pure vocational job-specific--their faculties had to include not only a wide variety of academic specialists but also a wide variety of instructors to teach the applied courses.[14] Thus, people with neither academic doctorates, masters, or even baccalaureate degrees were increasingly drawn from business, industry, the professions, and even the crafts to teach in the changing junior colleges. Consequently, the staffing of the traditional first and second year liberal arts and sciences courses also began to be affected. This raised such questions as to why a Ph.D. in English should be a prerequisite for teaching freshman and sophomore English in a junior college.[15] In contrast, persons with perhaps no degree at all were being hired to teach courses in such areas as drafting and auto mechanics.[16] Similar variances from traditional educational backgrounds began to appear in other curricular areas in the junior colleges.

With the passage of time a basic change in how the American society valued knowledge led to demands for changes in the curriculums of many junior colleges. These demands involved a growing emphasis in the instrumental valuing of knowledge. Since the public junior colleges evolved to a large degree within public school districts, they were less likely to have their curriculums strongly controlled by their faculties. The net effect of this lack of internal institutional control of curriculum was that societal demands for curriculum changes were more readily and rapidly accommodated. Subsequently, increasing numbers of practical and applied courses were offered. These changes in curriculum emphasis in the junior colleges, from one of a basically intrinsic valuing of knowledge to an emphasis on an instrumental valuing of knowledge, subsequently began to influence the curriculums of the four-year colleges and universities.

Demands of an economic nature also began to be made upon junior colleges. One of these was the economic reality that it was more costly to hire Ph.D.-level faculty members than those possessing lesser academic degrees or having no degrees at all. Because of a lack of adequate finances, due in part to low tuition, the junior colleges found it necessary to hire less academically prepared people for their faculties than those normally found in four-year colleges and universities. As a consequence, some four-year institutions began to seriously question the quality of the education that prospective transfer students were getting at the junior colleges.

The Junior/Community College Faculty

Today, confusion abounds as to exactly what junior colleges and the more recent community colleges have in common with four-year institutions, particularly traditional research-based universities. The confusion is notably apparent in the fundamental differences existing between the faculties of junior/community colleges and universities. One of these differences is clearly illustrated by the fact that, unlike most junior/community colleges, the hiring of new faculty members in a traditional university is strongly predicated on an evaluation of a candidate's published research and/or creative work. Although one's background in teaching and service is likely to be given some consideration for a university faculty position, the quality of published research and/or creative work is the primary factor considered in hiring faculty at universities with traditional academic structures. Once at the university the new faculty member is fully expected and, in fact, required to engage in research in order to gain tenure and promotion in rank. Even though good teaching might be considered to some degree, it is not valued nearly as high as research. In other words, it is extremely unlikely that a high level of productivity in research would be outweighed by or even equated with even an "outstanding" teaching evaluation.[17]

The emphasis on research in universities likewise can be explained in terms of the intrinsic/instrumental model for valuing knowledge. That is, the university is inherently dedicated to the development and enhancement of knowledge. This is reflected in its intrinsic valuing of knowledge. Such knowledge is not limited by either the prospective use of it or the perceived need for it. Yet, the knowledge-valuing environment present in the professional schools within universities is similar to the general perception of the value of knowledge in the vocational programs in the newer junior/community colleges. That is, the junior/community college is now committed, to a large extent, to the transmission of "useful" knowledge. This reflects an instrumental valuing of knowledge. Inherent in such a view is that most knowledge is justified by its perceived need and/or use. This becomes especially significant since in educational institutions it is the prevailing perception of knowledge that permeates and thus significantly influences their academic structures and technologies.

The dominant influence of the instrumental valuing of knowledge in the junior/community colleges has caused serious distortions in many traditional academic roles. This is evident, for example, in the role of the "professor" in junior/community colleges. Clearly, the titles of "assistant professor," "associate professor," and "professor" that have been adopted by junior/community college faculties were derived from the university. Yet, in the university the use of the initial title, "assistant professor," is predicated upon a strong research potential. In universities, the subsequent designations of "associate professor" and "professor" are, in fact, awarded only to those who have demonstrated superior achievement in research and/or creative productivity. What is more, the very essence of an assistant professor even becoming an associate professor is most likely to depend on concurrently being awarded tenure. Without tenure, of course, assistant professors are likely forced to eventually leave the institution.

On the other hand, the requisites of research or creative productivity are generally not considered to be the primary factors in either obtaining a position or in gaining tenure/promotion in junior/community colleges. Yet this state of affairs does not inhibit the junior/community colleges from using either the traditional faculty ranks or the rank-promotion concepts associated with universities. In addition, junior/community colleges also use a plethora of administrative ranks, course titles, and curricular designations traditionally found in the university.

The consequences of the junior/community colleges borrowing the traditional university labels has led to a confusion of much greater proportions. For example, when tenure and/or promotion and salary increases are at issue in junior/community colleges, the research function is clearly not emphasized, whereas the teaching function is. This is consistent with that emphasized at the elementary and high school level. Thus, on the one hand, both junior/community college and university faculty members are called "professor," yet on the other hand, they are hired for fundamentally different reasons. Since the role and functions of a professor in a university is distinctly different from a "professor" in a junior/community college, then the use of the title "professor" in a junior/community college is clearly a contradiction.

At this point it should be remembered that it was in the academic structure of the traditional university where the title of "professor" became associated with scholarly inquiry being directed toward the furthering of knowledge. The use of the title "professor" by the junior/community college is therefore inconsistent with the traditional meaning of the term as it had evolved prior to the advent of the junior/community college. If junior/community colleges are to be consistent with the historical and literal meaning of the language developed to describe the academic structures of universities, then they must logically expect their faculties to advance knowledge through scholarly inquiry by conducting basic research or doing significantly creative works. This, of course, is not the case. On the other hand, since the faculties of junior/community colleges engage primarily in functions similar to those of public school teachers, then the use of the title "teacher" in place of "professor" would be more logical. An analogous case can be made for other university labels being presently used by the junior/community colleges.

Language and Institutional Legitimacy

The illogical and inconsistent use of university institutional designations or labels by junior/community colleges has done more than just arouse semantic curiosity. It also has contributed to the confusion that abounds in regard to both the students they serve and the societal environment in which they exist. In some cases, at least, this confusion generally has given students attending junior/community colleges the false impression that they indeed are receiving the first two years of a baccalaureate-degree education equivalent to that offered by a university. That this false impression exists is more than just a remote possibility. Although junior/community colleges students do not often have an unusually difficult time passing the next level of courses in their respective academic areas when they get to the university,[18] they nonetheless are fully exposed to the "culture of inquiry" inherent in the academic milieu of the university for only two years instead of four. The end result is that these transfer students logically are less inclined to acquire an adequate sense of the importance of scholarly inquiry, the basis for a truly liberal education.

This is especially true for those students pursuing degrees in the arts and sciences.

In regard to professional school programs, the prerequisite courses taken at junior/community colleges are more appropriate to transfer to four-year colleges and universities. But the situation becomes less clear when junior/community college students take courses which either have no counterparts of or are not prerequisites for courses in baccalaureate degree programs. It can therefore be concluded that the strong instrumental valuing of knowledge present in junior/community colleges is not representative of predictable success on behalf of their students transferring to universities. What is needed instead are clarification of junior/community college curriculums, faculty preparation, faculty expectations, and their lack of emphasis on inquiry, these being the heart of the intrinsic valuing of knowledge. Such a clarification might in turn lead to a strengthening of the institutional legitimacy of both the university and the junior/community college within the environment of the broader society.

8. Contradictions In High School Teacher Preparation

The societal role of high school teachers has been historically clouded with confusion. In part, this confusion stems from the general misunderstanding of the differences between the institutional roles of high school teachers and university professors. Generally, the institutional role of the high school teacher is viewed as being parallel to that of the university professor, albeit at a different level. High school English teachers, for example, are generally considered to have an educational knowledge base of English exceeded only by that of professors of English. But when it comes to the actual teaching of English, high school teachers are confronted with a wide range of contradictions with which professors of English need not contend.

Much like university professors, high school teachers are expected to teach a body of knowledge. But unlike university professors, society expects high school teachers to be responsive to a myriad of both real and perceived student needs and concerns--many of which are not of a purely academic nature. This is compounded by the fact that high school teachers, unlike university professors, must teach students that are compelled by law to attend their classes. Because of these societal expectations and related legal constraints, the institutional role of high school teachers often includes, for example, (1) taking into consideration individual abilities, motivations, and behavioral and emotional problems of students; (2) being a "counselor" to students for a variety of personal as well as educational matters; (3) being an "advisor" or "sponsor" for extra curricular activities; and, most importantly, (4) teaching a particular body of knowledge in a manner consistent with the philosophy of the school, regardless of what knowledge the teacher might value and specifically how it should be taught. Since most of these teaching functions are not required of university professors, then the question arises as to just which university experiences have direct implications for the role that prospective high school teachers will be expected to fulfill.[19]

Professors as Models for High School Teachers

It is of no small consequence that university professors in the liberal arts and sciences serve as primary teaching role models for prospective high school teachers immediately prior to the high school teachers assuming teaching responsibilities in the public schools.[20] Like all university students, those aspiring to become high school teachers must acquire a body of knowledge. In "acquiring a body of knowledge" students literally "take" their academic degrees. The concept of "taking" one's academic degree is not totally symbolic. Rather, it is the "taking" of the knowledge that professors freely profess. Professors "profess" fields of knowledge essentially by publishing research, presenting papers at scholarly meetings, and teaching. Individual professors involve students directly in some or all of these activities. Likewise, as part of their university courses, professors require students to do considerable research and present their findings in extended oral and/or written discourse. Thus, the knowledge gained by university students from their professors is a product of all of the personal academic activities of professors and the mirroring of these activities in classes taught by professors. This is considerably unlike the knowledge gained by high school students from high school teachers. The single most important difference is one endemic to all university knowledge-acquiring activities; this is *scholarly inquiry*.

Because scholarly inquiry lies at the very core of the university ideal, university professors have particular expectations of their students. From the perspective of the professors, students must develop the skills and the spirit of scholarly inquiry in order to be fully educated. Thus, at the university, simply knowing "facts" will not singly qualify as a legitimate education. Likewise, there are many factors that affect the quality of not only the knowledge gained by the student but also the skills and attitudes needed in order to continue learning. Such factors include previous academic preparation, academic ability, time and motivation, and access to such resources as library holdings, laboratory equipment, and similar factors. Clearly, university professors might be particularly concerned with many of these factors, but the professors are neither required nor expected to take them into consideration when evaluating whether students have or have not acquired a body of knowledge. The acquiring of knowledge is solely the responsibility of the students. That is, regardless of any inhibiting factors that might exist, students are expected to "take" the knowledge professed by the professors.

Although an analysis of the differences between high school teachers and university professors can be conducted on many levels, the legal and instructional levels reveal the sharpest differences. While these differences might appear to be the most obvious, they are also likely to be the most misunderstood. As discussed above, both high school teachers and university professors are expected to teach fields of knowledge. But the broader society, and high school teachers themselves, often lack a clear understanding of the differences between the knowledge-dispensing institutional roles of high school teachers and university professors. For high school teachers, this lack of role clarification reveals significant contradictions that, in turn, present dilemmas they must attempt to resolve in their daily practice of teaching. To compound these dilemmas, some of the mitigating factors that account for the differences between the teaching roles of high school teachers and university professors are grounded in law.

One of the more significant legal factors that accounts for the differences between the roles of high school teachers and university professors is that public schools must accept all individuals who have been defined by law as eligible students. In general, it can logically be concluded that if states require, by law, that children attend school, then the states expect their public schools to provide suitable learning environments for these children. These expectations, in turn, limit the potential range of educational experiences that could possibly be provided for students, regardless of how these experiences are perceived by either teachers, students, or parents. Part of the contradiction for high school teachers here is that no parallel legal demands are placed on universities or institutions of higher education. Thus, high school teachers are faced with the contradiction of being responsible for imparting knowledge without being able to control many of the important factors that affect the imparting of knowledge. On the other hand, university professors can legally (through broad interpretations of academic freedom, for example) either significantly affect or completely ignore important variables that influence the imparting of knowledge at any or all levels.

In terms of instructional differences, university professors historically have not been compelled to be accountable for following any specific set of instructional guidelines. In fact, the strong role which academic freedom plays in universities permits broad leeway as to (1) what domains of knowledge a professor can explore in order to "know" and (2) how a professor actually goes about acquiring and transmitting that knowledge. Among other things, factors permitting university professors broad leeway in matters of instruction include the prerogative of the professor to choose textbooks, select library resources, determine laboratory procedures, use personally developed materials, and require students to participate in collaborative research. On the other hand, when examining the instructional discretion of teachers in most contemporary public high schools, it is readily apparent that these and other instructional aspects are much more tightly controlled.

Curricular and Methodological Contradictions

By successfully engaging in the total range of academic experiences within a university, a student earns a degree. In the broad sense, the experiences necessary to earn an academic degree are common for virtually all university students. But many of these experiences present a series of both knowledge and methodological contradictions for students who are preparing to be teachers in the public schools. These contradictions concern the answers to fundamental questions that pertain to what knowledge is to be taught by the teacher, to whom and where it will be taught, and the nature of the environments in which it will be taught.

The attitudes of high school teachers about what to teach, in regard to that which they acquired through their university experience, might be inconsistent with what society, the school, and parents expects them to teach. Likewise, the range of what they teach might be expected to vary greatly at any one given level both between schools and even within the same schools. For example, history and political science are each separate and major academic areas of study at the university, but at the high school level these academic areas often become integrated into "social studies." Likewise, at the university the study of any aspect or period of history is significantly more in-depth than that in the broader social studies curriculums found in most schools.

In addition, the wide differences in the curriculums of the various grade levels within public schools can be contradictory to the expectations of new teachers. For example, on the one hand language arts at the elementary school level is expected somehow to be related to English (and perhaps even foreign languages) at the high school level. But, on the other hand, the teaching of English in a high school is likely to have a vastly different set of expectations than the teaching of "language arts" in an elementary school. Such differences reflect the deeply ingrained ideological foundations of Progressive Education and the "core" curriculum that were introduced into the American public schools during the 1930s. This view of knowledge and its concomitant relationship to the academic structure of elementary schools are in sharp contrast to the highly valued traditional subject matter emphasis that prevails in the high schools despite massive attempts to restructure them academically.[21] But these different ideological views of knowledge and academic structures existing within the same institution--elementary through high school public education--are not the only contradictions with which future teachers had to contend.

The differences between elementary and high school grades are even further dichotomized when the "quality" of knowledge is considered. For example, society traditionally views the knowledge of English taught at the university level to be superior to that taught at the high school level, which in turn is considered to be superior to that taught at the elementary school level. In other words, whatever the level of preparation of teachers, elementary or high school, a vast range of societal expectations relating to the value of knowledge shapes the functions of public school teaching. These societal expectations are evident in the politically determined requirements for teaching credentials. The values reflected in these requirements are epistemological in that they are directly related to the ideological view about the structure and content of knowledge and the methods used to teach that knowledge. Because of the political nature of public education, the require-ments for teaching credentials are relative to any given historical period. Also, differences between what teachers expect their role to be and what it must actually be will further depend on both the kind of school for the same subject taught and the grade level at which the subject is taught. Although the forgoing analysis of the role expectations of public school teachers generally is somewhat simplistic, the role expectations for prospective high school teachers are far more complex.

Social and Cultural Issues

The differences in the social and cultural environments of the university and the broader society present significant contradictions for prospective high school teachers. For instance, high school teachers are more likely to teach in public schools having socioeconomic and cultural environments that are more diverse than those of most universities. Some of these socioeconomic and cultural differences are reflected in the parental aspirations for students in these public schools. One of the more critical ones is that many parents who are college graduates will do a great deal to insure that their children will also acquire a college degree. Paradoxically, parents with lower levels of education are generally more likely to have lower expectations for the educational attainment of their children. Under these circumstances, no matter how highly teachers value knowledge they cannot realistically expect all students to value knowledge in a similar fashion.

On the other hand, unlike the public high schools, which directly reflect the socioeconomic and cultural diversity of the broader society, the university, by its selection process of both students and faculty, is not affected by similar societal influences. The result is that the environment of the university has a much more homogeneous value orientation, particularly about education. The common bond within the social and cultural environment of the university is the high value placed simply on "knowing." Accordingly, students strive for a common goal, the academic degree; this signifies to the broader society that they are bona fide *knowers* of the knowledge of their respective fields. Thus, university faculties share in this experience in that, through scholarly inquiry, they join with students in a quest to learn even more. But contradictions immediately surface for the new high school teachers when they find that not all, if any, of their students generally share in the intrinsic valuing of learning that they experienced at the university.[22] This contradiction in the valuing of knowledge becomes even sharper for high school teachers when they find themselves faced with the prospects of university graduate study while, at the same time, teaching in the high school.

Graduate Study and Teaching

In many public school districts teachers must acquire graduate degrees in order to qualify for salary increases, additional certifications, and/or administrative and supervisory positions. But, in order to earn graduate degrees students must demonstrate the ability to independently conduct at least a modicum of scholarly research. Some of the more rigorous graduate degree programs also require in-depth research demonstrated through a thesis, dissertation, or the like. For the graduate students who are teachers in the public schools, it is not clearly known what the value is of extensive independent research experiences. What is known is that in their day-to-day practice of teaching they are faced with many problems not directly related to the academic subjects they are to teach.

Thus, the values about knowledge that public school teachers might acquire from their graduate studies could paradoxically pose fundamental contradictions. For instance, a high school English teacher who has completed extensive graduate study in English might also have to deal with high school students that are simply unmotivated to learn any English. When confronted with such students the teacher might, in some way, help them to merely "pass" the course. But, in simply getting a passing grade these students might not develop insights into the benefits of intrinsically valuing the knowledge of English. One consequence of this could be that these students might not succeed in English courses at the university where knowledge is valued intrinsically. Thus, the failure of the high school English teacher to at least begin to instill an intrinsic value of English in the students going on to the university would probably cast the teacher in a bad light. This would be especially true among those parents having high expectations for their children to succeed at the university. On the other hand, a stress on the intrinsic worth of English could result in inadequately helping those students who simply want to no more than pass high school English. In this case the teacher would risk severe parental and certainly administrative criticisms. Given even these comparatively simple paradoxical situations that confront high school teachers, it is logical to conclude that the complex role of a high school teacher is replete with contradictions.

Teaching Roles and Levels of Schooling

Although, as noted above, the differences between university and high school teaching are profound, those between university and elementary school teaching are even greater. Likewise, there are considerable differences between the roles of elementary and high school teachers. For instance, the respective levels of maturation of a seven-year old elementary school child and a seventeen-year old high school senior clearly necessitate significant variations in teaching roles. It should also be noted that there is considerably less variance in the roles of individual teachers within elementary schools than there is between the individual roles of teachers in high schools. But since the focus of this discussion is on high school teaching and university preparation, there need be little elaboration here of the role differences between elementary and secondary teachers. On the other hand, the broad continuum of role expectations of teachers at the high school level demand further consideration.

The different role expectations of high school teaching emanate, in part, from (1) societal beliefs about the organizational structure of schools, (2) the philosophical differences about curriculum between high schools, and (3) other curricular differences between and among courses taught in any particular high school. In light of the contradictions apparent among such factors as (1) the legal structure of the public schools, (2) differences in the nature of university and public school teaching, (3) inherent differences among high schools and courses, and (4) the stress on independent research at the university level, serious questions can be raised as to whether the preparation of high school teachers should even take place in a university environment.

Implications of Theory for Practice

It is logical to conclude that to learn in one way about the act of teaching, yet to be required by societal norms and circumstances to actually teach in a significantly different way, implies a set of theoretical guidelines for practices which must clearly be distinguishable from each other. That is, ideally, a teacher should know about and be able to use theories and models of teaching behaviors which can be isomorphically transposed to the public school setting. Thus, the question here is whether "learning about" teaching is equivalent to, or more appropriate for, successful teaching than acquiring extensive and purposeful "experience in" teaching.[23] In fact, the ideal of professional preparation is grounded largely in the importance of experience. If public school teaching is to be considered a professional activity in the classical sense of the concept, then a question arises as to whether the preparation of teachers can be done effectively at the university. In short, can the total university experience provide an adequate set of real, vicarious, and/or simulated teaching experiences which would enable prospective teachers to learn about teaching, engage in the practice of teaching, and be evaluated for future competence in teaching?

That the consequences of such university programs might not always be fully predictable should not necessarily make those programs suspect. At the same time, care must be taken that university programs designed to prepare people for entrance into specific professions are not made so occupationally oriented that they lose their intrinsic academic character. After all, physicians do not learn the practice of medicine solely through methods of "trial-and-error." They first engage in significant study of medical procedures and processes in light of their theoretical, historical, and ethical development. Similarly, prospective high school teachers of English, history, or mathematics would not be adequately prepared if they went into the schools to teach without first having the knowledge of the theoretical, historical, and ethical perspectives of these academic subjects. If indeed the opposite were true, then prospective high school teachers, as well as physicians and other professionals, for that matter, would save society considerable resources by returning to the earlier apprenticeship method of preparing people for the professions. Since no state any longer certifies teachers solely by an apprenticeship-teaching experience, then it is clear that the broader society does in fact highly value certain elements in the university experience of future teachers.

Common Values of the University Experience

There theoretically is at least one common or core belief present at all levels of all university academic programs. In a general sense, this belief is deeply held by university professors. The essence of this common belief is, not surprisingly, that knowledge should be valued for its own sake, that is, intrinsically. The intrinsic valuing of knowledge is not open to justification solely by need and/or use. It is not instrumental. The intrinsic valuing of knowledge is expressed fully in the spirit of inquiry, for it is in inquiring about the truth that the value of knowing becomes most fundamental. In the university, the intrinsic valuing of knowledge has long been championed by faculties of arts and sciences, it being deeply ingrained over many centuries in the cultural fabric of these faculties. The position taken here is that because of its liberating nature, the intrinsic valuing of knowledge should be more tightly woven into the structures of all academic areas of the university, especially those of schools of education. The reasons that this becomes particularly important for prospective high school teachers are manifold. These include the fact that the high school students they will be teaching are in transition to adulthood and thus will soon be eligible for full participation in the political processes of citizenship. Also, almost half of those students who graduate from high school will attend an institution of higher education where the likelihood of valuing knowledge intrinsically is greater than in the broader society.

9. Contradictions in Elementary and Junior/Middle School Teacher Education in the University

University students who want to be teachers in elementary or junior high/middle schools face a different set of problems in their eventual practice than the problems faced by high school teachers. But, like the problems faced by prospective high school teachers, those faced by prospective elementary and junior high/middle school teachers are also rooted in contradictions inherent in their preparation programs. The reasons for this are to a large degree political in that these programs reflect teacher licensing and certification standards which are under almost constant revision by state governments.

Teacher licensing/certification standards are established through an elaborate political process culminating in specific legislative mandates or guidelines having direct connections to university preparation programs. For example, to be certified as a high school teacher most states require the candidate to have a major or near-major in at least one academic field of study. On the other hand, to be certified as an elementary school teacher one does not have to have a special academic major. Although common, this dual standard is not uniform for all states. A state that departs significantly from the typical dual certification standards for high school and elementary teachers is California. The California standards provides for a unified K-12 lifetime certificate for all teachers.[24]

Regardless of their specific requirements, state mandated teacher certification standards clearly have a profound effect on the structure of academic programs of teacher preparation institutions. The greatest effect is usually found in the academic structures of schools or departments of education, particularly in states where dual certification standards exist.

Contrasting Elementary and High School
Teacher Preparation Programs

The baccalaureate programs of prospective secondary teachers are usually composed of a majority of courses in the arts and sciences. Included in the array of arts and sciences courses is at least one block of courses that nearly or totally constitutes an academic major in a particular field of knowledge other than education. In fact, to be certified as a secondary school teacher one need not have a baccalaureate degree in secondary education. In most states a student can earn an arts and sciences degree with a major in a particular discipline and meet certification requirements by taking as electives the few courses needed in education. In either case, be it a baccalaureate degree in secondary education or in an academic area in the arts and sciences with education courses as electives, it is clear that arts and sciences courses predominate in secondary teacher preparation programs.

In sharp contrast to high school teacher preparation programs, traditional arts and sciences courses make up only about one-half of most elementary school teacher preparation programs. In fact, most baccalaureate degree programs for prospective elementary school teachers require that about fifty percent of the total credit hours consist of specific courses in education. To some extent many of these required education courses, interestingly enough, resemble arts and sciences courses both in certain aspects of their content and in their titles. For example, a course called "Elementary School Science" might have selected bits of content from a variety of physical and biological science courses found in colleges of arts and sciences. Analogous examples can also be found in such courses as "language arts," "social studies," and in music courses offered by departments of elementary education.

What is significant here is that the academic areas that are represented collectively in elementary teacher preparation programs are conversely represented individually in secondary teacher preparation programs. For example, courses in "social studies" in a department of elementary education are intended to acquaint future elementary school teachers with the content of the social sciences and related areas traditionally found in colleges of arts and sciences. Unlike prospective elementary school teachers who take broad courses in "social studies" from professors of elementary education, prospective secondary school teachers must take specific courses in most or all of the separate academic areas. These include specific courses in history, political science, sociology, anthropology, economics, and the like, as taught by professors of these academic areas.

What is important for the discussion here is the fact that in universities, elementary education courses, with arts and sciences-like characteristics and titles, are most often taught by professors in departments of elementary education rather than by professors in the various academic departments of the arts and sciences. In fact, university elementary education departments often have professors who specialize in such areas as elementary school social studies, science, language arts, music, and perhaps other academic areas parallel to those in the arts and sciences. Thus the inescapable question arises as to just what it means to be a professor of "elementary school science," for example. Since science is so broad and includes such specific areas of inquiry as physics, chemistry, and biology, among others, it would be unrealistic to assume that a professor of "elementary school science" has a knowledge base equivalent to the sum total of the professors of each of the specific academic disciplines of science. Of course, the same questions can be raised about the other courses taught in departments of elementary education that parallel academic fields in the arts and sciences. These questions are particularly important when one considers that most faculty members of university departments of elementary education themselves most likely majored in elementary education at the undergraduate level. It would be unusual, indeed, to find one who has an advanced degree in any one specific academic area in the arts and sciences, much less in several of these areas.

Knowledge Perspectives of Professors of Elementary Education

The difference in preparation of elementary education professors in such broad areas as science, language arts, and social studies generally varies greatly from that of their counterparts in the arts and sciences disciplines. Among these are differences in perspectives about knowledge and the resulting differences in attitudes towards such knowledge. Generally, the educational ideology of elementary school "social studies" professors is one which primarily focuses on the total life of the elementary school child, rather than just on the subject matter. In the field of education this ideology is described as being that of the "whole child." To professors of elementary education, "social studies," as well as other arts and sciences fields, are simply viewed as elements of the child's development within society. This "holistic" view of the child as a functioning and inseparable part of society is subsequently transferred to the subject matter. Thus, subject matter is also viewed holistically and appears in the elementary school curriculums in such broad areas as "social studies" instead of history, political science, economics, and sociology; "science" instead of physics, chemistry, and biology; and "language arts" instead of English, literature, and speech.

The binding together of academic areas into new entities has in turn created more issues in regard to the valuing of knowledge. For example, the separate academic disciplines that constitute elementary school "social studies" lose the significant nuances which initially gave rise to these individual fields in the arts and sciences. Over time, the idea that a variety of separate academic areas logically can be bound together into a single entity called "social studies" has been fully institutionalized as a rational myth within the broader society. Likewise, these newly evolved disciplines-unto-themselves are widely believed by many public school educators to be those in which professors of elementary education can actually specialize.

At times, specialization on the part of the elementary social studies professor does entail more in-depth study of separate arts and sciences disciplines. Preparation for the doctorate in elementary social studies, nevertheless, does not resemble, and certainly does not require, separate doctoral dissertations in such specific academic areas as history, political science, sociology, and economics. Thus, because of the nature of the academic preparation of professors of elementary school "social studies," the social sciences background for prospective elementary school teachers consists largely of courses in "social studies." Rarely if ever do these programs require separate arts and sciences majors or even large numbers of courses in any of the academic disciplines which elementary school "social studies" is to represent. Historically, this state of affairs has largely reflected the transition of elementary teacher preparation from the normal school to the university.

Implications for Junior High School Instruction

When moving from the elementary school to the junior high school, students are confronted by many significant changes in both the structure of their educational experiences and the organizational environment in which they must function. In the elementary school the student is in an environment dominated by the "whole child" educational ideology.[25] This view of the child is reinforced by teachers and administrators through the curriculum and practically every other aspect of the school. But, in the junior high school the educational structure and environment are radically different. These differences are both quantitative and qualitative. Included among these are (1) having several teachers each day, (2) going to different rooms each period, and among others, (3) having more male teachers. In general, many of these experiences for the new junior high school students are very unlike any they had during their elementary school years. But of all of these differences the most significant is the unique composition of the faculty and the attitudes of the individual teachers toward knowledge and its relationship to education.

Unlike both the elementary schools that have teachers prepared exclusively in elementary education, and the high schools that have teachers prepared exclusively for secondary education, junior high school teachers can claim no unique preparation program. Most junior high school faculties have a mixture of both elementary and high school teachers. This is particularly noteworthy when considering the contrast in the attitudes towards knowledge that elementary and high school teachers reflect in their practices as a result of the differences in their respective preparation programs.

Junior High School Faculties

As noted previously, the most significant aspect of the academic preparation of high school teachers is that a specialization is required in at least one of the arts and sciences disciplines. But such specialization often presents significant curriculum and programming problems at the high school level. One such problem is that newly certified teachers in fields like physics, chemistry, or biology often find it difficult to obtain a teaching position exclusively in one of these fields unless they find positions in very large high schools. Since the majority of the nearly 24,000[26] high schools in the United States have enrollments that preclude offering no more than one and at most a few sections of physics, for example, then a physics teacher would also be required to teach such classes as "general science." In addition, one result of the frequently changing grade-organization patterns of schools since the mid-1800s[27] is that many high school teachers, regardless of their academic specialties, often must teach in junior high schools. These schools usually include grade levels that range from grades five or six to grades eight or nine.

But, once in the junior high schools, teachers prepared as high school physics teachers, for example, will be expected to teach "general" science, rather than physics.[28] Despite teaching "general science" rather than teaching physics exclusively, these teachers will continue to intrinsically value the knowledge in their major academic area of physics. The educational environment of the junior high school becomes even more confusing for students when they are confronted by analogous faculty staffing in the separate "social studies" and "language arts" courses. When combined with the differences in organizational structure, beginning junior high school students do indeed face many serious contradictions.

Contradictions Confronting
Junior High School Students

Junior high school students are faced with many contradictions because their new educational environment has little resemblance to the familiar, logically consistent, and emotionally comfortable "whole child" environment of the elementary school. Perhaps the most perplexing of these contradictions are those that are related to the intrinsic versus the instrumental valuing of knowledge. As noted above, the junior high school students are confronted by these different valuing of knowledge perspectives because they will likely have some teachers that have been prepared to teach in elementary schools and others that have been prepared to teach in high schools. Likewise, the effect of a "junior" high school organizational structure as a transition for elementary school students to high school years presents many contradictions. These changes in structure come at the same time that most preadolescents and adolescents are experiencing significant social, psychological, and physical changes. Consequently, it is indeed difficult for children to adjust to a dramatically different educational environment at this critical stage in their lives. The dilemmas posed by these contradictions often are reflected in student behaviors that have characteristics of a cultural shock.

The "Middle" School

As discussed earlier, the sharpness in the differences between the "whole child" educational environment of the elementary school and the "subject matter" environment of the high school can be explained by how knowledge is valued. These differences become evident in the nature of the traditional junior high schools faculties. Granted, the sharpness of this shift of focus from "child"- to "subject"-centered might be debatable. But what is factual are the fundamental academic differences between university baccalaureate degree programs for elementary school teachers and high school teachers. Likewise, what is also evident is the almost complete absence of any unique university degree programs to prepare teachers specifically for the traditional junior high schools.

With few exceptions the intrinsic valuing of knowledge inherent in the arts and sciences, as reflected in secondary teacher licensing/certification, essentially runs counter to the instrumental valuing of knowledge emphasized in most elementary teacher licensing/certification standards. The fact that both elementary and secondary certified teachers were present in traditional junior high schools clearly affected the character of the teaching which confronted the new junior high school students. Thus, as argued earlier, the educational structures of the traditional junior high schools inherently contain fundamental contradictions related to the valuing of knowledge. These contradictions often present irresolvable dilemmas for junior high school students. As a result of trying to remedy some of the psychological and social problems associated with the concept of a "junior" high school experience for pre-adolescents, the now ubiquitous "middle" school was ostensibly conceived.[29]

Although there is no agreed-upon "best" pattern, middle schools typically include one or two grades above and/or below grade seven.[30] What is more, the middle school movement prompted some states to establish unique certification standards for middle school teachers. It should further be noted that the more recent modification of the structure of the elementary-junior-senior high school programs has not likely changed the basic nature of the educational milieu of the pupils.

Academic Background of Teacher Educators

The differences in preparation of teachers at the elementary, junior high/middle school, and high school levels can also be assessed in terms of the specialization of faculty members in the college or university which the teachers attended. For instance, it is not unusual for those expecting to be certified as high school teachers to not only have more specialized arts and sciences courses in their respective teaching fields but also to have an arts and sciences faculty member in that field as their teaching mentor. The latter indeed becomes the case when a jointly-appointed professorship exists between the secondary education department and the respective teaching field department(s) in the arts and sciences. Common examples of this are professors who have joint appointments in either biology and education, English and education, mathematics and education, and history and education, among others. On the other hand, joint appointments occur far less frequently between a department of elementary education and the college of arts and sciences. A notable departure from this exists in "music education," since these programs usually focus on the teaching of music across the entire K-12 grade span. But the consequences of the joint-appointment approach in preparing secondary school teachers are profoundly different from the comprehensive role of the elementary education professor in preparing future elementary school teachers. The fact that joint appointments predominate at the secondary level, yet rarely exist at the elementary level, is reflected in that elementary teachers generally value knowledge instrumentally rather than intrinsically.

It is of little wonder why teacher preparation for the elementary school level is subject to so many criticisms. One of the primary criticisms is that many of these programs do not attempt to foster within the prospective elementary school teachers an intrinsic appreciation of an academic field of study. Instead, the programs focus on pedagogical issues and methods which tend to promote an instrumental valuing of any and all knowledge. Other criticisms question whether elementary school teachers have an adequate knowledge of specific course content in order to be able to effectively teach subjects such as math, science, and social studies. Still others are directed at university faculties that staff elementary teacher preparation programs. What is generally inherent in these criticisms is the assumption that, unlike professors in the arts and sciences, elementary education professors lack an interest in the traditional pursuit of fundamental knowledge. This assumption implies that elementary education professors are less likely to value fundamental knowledge intrinsically. The result of these criticisms is a general lack of academic respect for education faculties *in toto*.

Unfortunately, the respective secondary education professors, what relatively few of them there are, also find little in common with elementary education professors. What is more, in schools of education where joint-appointments in secondary education and the arts and sciences do exist, the conflicts between secondary and elementary education professors are likely to be intensified. Finally, internal differences in elementary and secondary teacher preparation within schools of education are further compounded by those education professors who claim to be K-12 "curriculum specialists."

Effects of Contradictions in
Teacher-Education Programs

What effects the fundamental contradictions inherent in teacher-education programs might have on both the ends and the means of these programs is not exactly clear, although they could be very disruptive. One particularly important effect involves the perception held by university faculties about schools of education. Because they have a significant elementary teacher preparation function--which has as its primary focus the "whole child" and not subject-matter content--schools of education are viewed almost schizophrenically by university faculties. For example, when viewed from a pragmatic level, arts and sciences faculties need education majors to enroll in their courses, regardless of why the students do so. Yet, when viewed from a philosophical level, the education students who enroll in arts and sciences courses are expected to value knowledge intrinsically, even though they have already acquired an instrumental valuing of knowledge from their course work education. To a large degree, then, one result of being placed in situations where they must deal with contradictions in the valuing of knowledge leads education majors to exhibit a distinctly different attitude about knowledge than do students majoring in the traditional arts and sciences. It is this distinctly different attitude about the valuing of knowledge that causes arts and sciences faculties to view education majors as somewhat less capable than arts and sciences majors.

Schools of education likewise reflect an analogous schizophrenia. Largely due to their instrumental valuing of knowledge in elementary education programs, schools of education must also deal with the contradictions inherent in their own academic structures. These contradictions are grounded in the inter-mediating facility of the traditional university professor whose intrinsic valuing of knowledge is inherent in the pursuit of any and all knowledge for its own sake. But the contradictions are brought more sharply into focus by those professors of education who, paradoxically, choose to value knowledge instrumentally.

NOTES

1. Although the Supreme Court of the United States has, on many occasions, reaffirmed this notion, its most famous clarification of what free speech means was made in 1943 by Justice Jackson when he wrote, "If there is any fixed star in our constitutional constellation, it is that no official, high or petty, can prescribe what shall be orthodox in politics, nationalism, religion, or *other matters of opinion* [Emphasis added] . . ." See *West Virginia State Board of Education v. Barnette*, 319 U.S. 624, 63 S.Ct. 1178, 87 L.Ed. 1628 (1943).

2. It is interesting to note that in Mississippi the junior colleges were an outgrowth of the county agriculture high school and were promoted as "the poor man's college." See Jesse Parker Bogue, *The Community College* (New York: McGraw-Hill, 1950), p. 86.

3. In regard to this distinction in names, it appears that, "During the 1950s and 1960s the term *junior college* was applied more often to the lower-division branches of private universities and to two-year colleges supported by churches or organized independently, while the term 'community college' came gradually to be used for comprehensive, publicly supported institutions. By the 1970s, the term *community college* was usually applied to both types." See Arthur M. Cohen and Florence B. Brawer, *The American Community College* (San Francisco: Jossey-Bass, 1982), p. 5.

4. See Frederick Rudolph, *The American College and University* (New York: Alfred A. Knopf, 1968), p. 463.

5. See Bogue, p. 86.

6. *Idid.*, p. 85.

7. It is interesting to note that in the early 1930s only about fifteen to twenty percent of the freshmen students would continue their education beyond the junior college. This percentage increased to twenty five percent in 1937 and thirty-three percent in 1952. See Leland L. Medsker, *The Junior College: Progress and Prospect* (New York: McGraw-Hill, 1960), pp. 89-93. For a brief history of the two-year college, see also, Clyde E. Blocker, Richard H. Plummer, and Richard C. Richardson, Jr., *The Two-Year College: A Social Synthesis* (Englewood Cliffs, New Jersey: Prentice-Hall, 1965), pp. 23-45. For a much earlier account of the junior college, see Leonard V. Koos, *The Junior-College Movement* (New York: Ginn and Company, 1925).

8. Increased enrollments in colleges were marked by broad shifts in their make-up, in that they were, "No longer sequestered enclaves operated apparently for the sons of the wealthy and educated on their way to positions in the professions and for their daughters of the same group, who would be marked with the manners of a cultured class; the colleges were opened to ethnic minorities, to lower-income groups, and to those whose prior academic performance had been marginal. And to all higher education institution, the community colleges contributed most to opening the system. Established in every metropolitan area, they were available to all comers, attracting the new student, the minorities, the women, the people who had done poorly in high school, those who would otherwise never have considered further education." See Cohen and Brawer, p. 19. Similarly, it has been pointed out that, "Compared to students in other sectors in higher education, those in community colleges are more likely to be, on average, less wealthy, members of minority groups, older, part-time, working, and less well-prepared. Not surprisingly, the student body of a typical community college is far more heterogeneous than that of a liberal arts college or university." See David W. Breneman and Susan C. Nelson, *Financing Community Colleges: Economic Perspective* (Washington, D.C.: The Brookings Institute, 1981), pp. 22-23.

9. In a study in the early 1920s it was concluded that a potent and perhaps predominant factor explaining why many students attended junior colleges and not colleges and universities away from home was, ". . . immaturity and parents' fears of its consequences . . ." See Koos, p. 173.

10. It should be noted that there was much debate about precisely what the junior college curriculum represented. Many viewed it simply as the extension of the high school, while others thought it more appropriately represented collegiate work. Some even proposed that the last two years of high school (grades 11 and 12) be combined with the first two years of college to form a "new American college." See John A. Sexon and John W. Harbeson, *The New American College* (New York: Harpers & Brothers, 1946).

11. This view has clearly been transferred to the community college. O'Connell has noted that, "Transfer programs in community colleges are set up specifically to educate freshmen and sophomores who plan to move on to four-year colleges or universities as bachelor's degree candidates when they have completed their first two years and have received an associate degree." See Thomas E. O'Connell, *Community Colleges: A President's View* (Urbana, Illinois: University of Illinois Press, 1968), p. 38. This ability to transfer to four-year institutions is clearly illustrated by the fact that at one point in the early 1960s over half of those in the upper classes of colleges and universities in California had spent their first two collegiate years in community colleges. See M. M. Chambers, "Diversify the Colleges," *Journal of Higher Education* 31 (1960): 10-13, cited in Rudolph, p. 487.

12. By 1958 it was reported that in the nineteen (19) state two-year colleges and six (6) state-supported agriculture and technical institutes in New York more than ninety percent (90%) of the 14,023 students enrolled were in technical terminal programs. See Medsker, p. 117.

13. See Koos, p. 232.

14. By the mid-1960s the idea of junior colleges offering both transfer and career programs was firmly entrenched in the structure of these institutions. For example, see Norman C. Harris, *Technical Education in the Junior College/New Programs for New Jobs* (Washington, D.C.: American Association of Junior Colleges, 1964), also cited in Thomas E. O'Connell, *Community Colleges: A President's View* (Urbana, Illinois: University of Illinois Press, 1968), pp. 42-43.

15. By the time that the junior college as an institution was almost completely transformed into the "community" college, Bushnell noted that, "The proliferation of new two-year colleges during the past decade has created a new market for instructors who are neither research-oriented nor necessarily committed to the single academic discipline. Despite the pronouncements of some authorities, most two-year college administrators are not seeking recent Ph.D.'s steeped in the traditions of graduate research. First and foremost, they want capable teachers." See David S. Bushnell, *Organizing for Change: New Priorities for Community Colleges* (New York: McGraw-Hill, 1973), p. 35.

16. In 1973 a study conducted on community colleges included characteristics of the faculty sampled. The study reported that, "Three out of four community/junior college faculty members have a master's degree. Five

percent completed a Ph.D. or Ed.D." Furthermore, the study revealed that, "Among the academic faculty, 90 percent have a master's degree or higher, while only 52 percent of the occupational faculty have reached this educational level. Many of the occupational faculty chose education as their profession after spending a number of years in another field, presumably one related to their area of specialization . . .. However, the gap between the education level of occupations instructors and those in the academic fields is being reduced, as almost half of the occupational faculty are currently enrolled in an advanced training program . . ." See Bushnell, pp. 32-33.

17. Regarding arguments comparing community college faculties to university faculties, Cohen and Brawer stated that, "This argument stems from a view of professionalism among university faculties that has ill suited teaching in the senior institutions, where, as faculty allegiance turned more to research, scholarship, and academic disciplinary concerns, interest in teaching waned." They stated further that a community college faculty does not have to be like a university faculty as it can develop along different lines. This would likely have to occur since it seems that, "The community college faculty disciplinary affiliation is too weak, the institution's demands for scholarship are practically nonexistent, and the teaching loads are too heavy for that form of professionalism to occur." Cohen and Brawer, p. 88.

18. See Bogue, pp. 74-76.

19. Although many aspects of university preparation programs for public school teachers are in contradiction to what will be expected of them in their future roles as either kindergarten, elementary, junior high/middle school, or high school teachers, the discussion here is limited solely to the contradictions at the high school level.

20. For a more complete discussion of this relationship, see Henry R. Weinstock, "On Valuing Knowledge Intrinsically in Secondary and Elementary Teacher Education," *Proceedings of the Southwestern Philosophy of Education Society* 34 (1984): 138.

21. Criticisms of this approach have been extensive. An example is one by the late Max Rafferty, an education critic of the 1970s, when he asked, "Is subject matter in your school paid lip service, but relegated to the back seat? Are things like social studies and language arts and orientation being taught instead of history and geography and English? If these things are being done, it doesn't much matter what they call it. What you've got is Progressivism." See Max Rafferty, "What Does Your Child Learn in School?," *St. Louis Globe Democrat* (17 November 1969): 14A.

22. For current in-depth discussions on teacher and student expectations, see, for example, Ernest Boyer, *High Schools: A Report on Secondary Education in America* (Princeton, New Jersey: Carnegie Foundation for the Advancement of Teaching, 1983).

23. According to Sykes, "The literature suggests that the claim to professional status rests upon the existence of a codified body of special knowledge, a community of practice joined by special ways of thinking, valuing, and acting, and the professional school which is required for their transmission. If the university is not essential to the growth of the knowledge base, if formal preparation is believed to be unnecessary, if knowledge is craft alone, then apprenticeship will be enough . . ." Gary Sykes, "Evolution of the Profession," *Forum*, the Holmes Group, No. 1 (1987): 11.

24. In California the "Teacher Preparation and Licensing Act of 1970" (the Ryan Act), reduced the number of credentials needed for teaching, eliminated academic versus non-academic distinctions between teaching majors, and made all teaching credentials applicable for grades K-12. See Peter L. LoPresti, "California: The Impact of the Commission on Teacher Preparation and Licensing," *Phi Delta Kappan* (May 1977): 675.

25. "In general, it may also be assumed that, at least in most public and many private elementary schools, the *whole child* concept of teaching prevails, that is, the entire (rather than only the intellectual) development of the child is recognized and is hence to be developed through the curricula comprising the preschool through the sixth grade levels." See Henry R. Weinstock, "On Valuing Knowledge Intrinsically in Secondary and Elementary Teacher Education," *Proceedings of the Southwestern Philosophy of Education Society* 34 (1984): 138.

26. Stephen J. Knezevich, *Administration of Public Education* (New York: Harper and Row, 1984), p. 173.

27. See Knezevich, pp. 324-25.

28. It is indeed rare to find any teachers that have been prepared as high school teachers teaching their academic specialties in junior high/middle schools.

29. Although the concept of the middle school was considered around the turn of the twentieth century, it had virtually disappeared during the 1930s. The concept again gained favor with educators during the 1950s. Although the growth was very slow, in 1966 New York City replaced all of its junior high schools with middle or intermediate schools. See, Knezevich, pp. 331-32. Since the 1960s interest has varied and peaked in the early 1970s when about 2000 middle schools were either newly established or former junior high

schools retitled. See Educational Research Service, *Summary of Research on Middle Schools* (Arlington, Virginia: Educational Research Service, 1975), 40 pp. Cited in Knezevich, p. 332. Also, exactly why many school districts have adopted the organizational structure (in name at least) of the "middle" school and abandoned that of the junior high school is not fully clear. Perhaps it is mere novelty. But it has been reported that the increased popularity of the middle school in the 1980s might be due to problems in the desegregation of schools. See Knezevich, p. 332.

30. Knezevich, pp. 331-32.

Four

Contradictions in the Valuing
of Knowledge

Overview

The public education movement in eighteenth-century Europe underscored the era of national systems of education. Concurrent with this movement was the resurgence of philosophical idealism. Prominent among those who championed a return to idealism was Immanual Kant (1724-1804), the noted German idealist philosopher. Kant stressed the importance of character education in the development of the spiritual side of the human being, namely moral capacity. Because the Kantian view is consistent with the concepts of both the liberated individual and the intrinsic valuing of knowledge, it is particularly important for the structuring of public education within the context of the American democracy.

Historically, two fundamental purposes have justified American public education. The first has been to provide each child with the requisite knowledge and skills to be a good citizen.[1] The second has been to benefit the child as an individual.[2] Initially, the first purpose was paramount. To fulfill this purpose it was important for education to be a "common" school experience. But by the beginning of the twentieth century the second purpose became increasingly more important. The "child benefit" view of education soon took on a "practical" or vocational dimension, especially for those considered to be socially disadvantaged. This was one of the outcomes of massive efforts to shape social policy through complex political struggles at all levels of government.

But social policy issues have always been intertwined with policies that shape and control the structures of American public education. Included among these social/educational policy issues are concerns about who should have access to various educational programs, who should determine what counts as knowledge in these educational programs, how the system of public education should be financed, and who should control educational policy itself. What is particularly pertinent for this discussion are the effects that public education has on social class structure. In this regard, the social inequities for the educationally disadvantaged are often compounded because certain educational policies have the effect of solidifying social class structures. Examples of such policies include the "outcome measurable" public education programs that have been mandated by many states today.

Public education policies that require an "outcome measurable" standard for academic programs are more likely to be championed by those from the middle and upper socioeconomic classes. This is understandable because it is in these social classes where the materialistic and narrow "bottom line" business management ideology has gained the widest acceptance and, subsequently, has permeated virtually every aspect of the lives of those in these classes. This is particularly evident in the institutions they control, including not only business and corporate enterprises but public institutions as well. It is this group, more than any other, that has had the political power to significantly influence virtually all social policy in America. There is ample evidence that outcomes of measurable education policies have spread to virtually all of public education today. This has come about even though serious contradictions exist between "outcome measurable" educational practices and the Constitutional ideals of social equality and equal educational access.

The contradictions between "outcome measurable" public school practices and democratic ideals become sharpened in light of the "separate but fair" justification of other policies that have shaped the fundamental structure of American public education along racial, social, gender, and economic class lines. For example, both the establishment of vocational schools in lower socioeconomic neighborhoods and "comprehensive" high schools in middle class neighborhoods are the result of public education policy shaped by a "separate but fair" rationale. These policies are particularly significant in that they are grounded in a questionable moral justification--at least for a liberal democratic society--that students from poorer families need a vocational education so they can "succeed" in life. But this view of educational "success" places virtually insurmountable barriers before children in the lower socioeconomic strata who want to pursue careers other than those of a vocational nature.

Likewise, serious contradictions between educational practices and American democratic ideals also exist within the context of private education. Although private schools, be they secular or religious, can exemplify both the ideals of private enterprise and quality education in a free democratic society,[3] they can also significantly influence the solidification of class structures, particularly through selective admissions policies.

Clearly, all social policies that further engender and perpetuate rigid class structures are evidence of the continued existence of ancient aristocratic and more modern bourgeois values within the culture of society as a whole. Because of their direct influence on the succeeding generations of a society, public education policies and practices that are based on the values of a social structure of domination undermine a fundamental principle which is at the very heart of American democratic ideal--equality of opportunity.

10. Intrinsically Valuing Knowledge and Individuality

Historically within American society, a variety of beliefs have existed about the legitimate role of public education. One common view, for example, is that public education is an effective means for promoting good citizenship. But regardless of what its idealized role should be, it can not be argued that public education has not played a major role in shaping the structure of American society. It has been such an important factor in the lives of most Americans that it is commonly believed to be an American invention. But the idea of universal public education was not conceived here in America. In the Western world, the movement for public education began in Europe during the 1700s where the roots of "national systems" of education first began to take hold.[4] Such factors as the Industrial Revolution, increased political fomentation, and the influence of science and technology on their economic systems began to significantly affect the need for nation-states to take the responsibility for the education of their citizenry. What is important to consider for this discussion is that the public education movement closely paralleled the resurgence of philosophical idealism.

Idealism and Modern Education

In the eighteenth century Immanuel Kant had strongly advocated that the primary function of education was to develop character through a continuing appraisal of one's moral freedom. But Kant had to deal with the evolving scientific movement, a *Weltanschauung* he would not completely deny despite the growing dominance of the determinism of the mechanistic materialists who grounded their beliefs in a scientific rationality. Kant took his position on education because he believed that the deterministic perspective of the materialists could not account for a view of individual freedom in one's moral life. The determinists reasoned that if the universe is governed in every way by laws and principles of science, then, as part of the universe the human being could also be explained by the laws and principles of science. Even to the idealist Kant the notion of a mechanistically determined universe seemed a reasonable way to deal with the world of space and time. But, he further reasoned, if such a deterministic world incorporates the individual human being, then a moral dilemma logically must exist. For Kant the nature of this dilemma was epistemological. To resolve this dilemma he postulated the existence of *noumenon* and *phenomenon*.

Kant viewed the world of *Ding-an-sich* as the *noumenal* world, one in which the ultimate causes of sense perceptions exist in and of themselves. He believed that access to noumenon can be gained only through intuition; thus, it is only through intuition that one gains access to an objective moral order. Kant further reasoned that access to noumenon gives a person the ability to maintain a moral life, so long as the individual chooses to be free. Thus, to Kant, an individual's choice to accept being free could only be maintained in the noumenal world.

Kant's conception of a *phenomenal* world revealed his concern about philosophy which during his time was rapidly being replaced by science as the primary way of understanding the world. But rather than rejecting science Kant instead relegated it to a useful though not ultimate way of describing reality. He reasoned that one's material experiences are the consequences of sense impressions, yet the causes of these sense impressions cannot ultimately be determined. This, of course, is opposite to the view that science is the sole way to describe the world of space and time.

Consequently, in separating ultimate reality from the world of space and time into the real world of noumenon and the experiential world of phenomenon, Kant essentially had postulated a dual human consciousness. To Kant, the awareness of the world of space and time was sense perception and the interpretation thereof was explainable through science. But, he reasoned, phenomenon does not explain all of reality because if it did, then there would be no free moral choosing. Kant further reasoned that the awareness of a much broader reality, one to which access can be gained through intuition, justifies the existence of noumenon. For Kant the choice was between either a world completely ordered but devoid of God, or a world which God oversees. He reasoned that since man was moral, and morality evidently presupposed God, then man must therefore be a moral being. Education for Kant thus entailed the development of the spiritual side of the human being, namely, moral capacity.[5]

Character Development and Education

For Kant, the primary purpose of education was the development of character. In light of this, there are certain aspects of the academic structure of American education today that appropriately lend themselves to an analysis from the frame of reference of Kant's noumenal/phenomenal view of the world. One such structural aspect is the relationship between the teacher and the student and to what proportion the teacher views the student as either noumenon or phenomenon at any given time.[6] The extent that a teacher permits the student to make significant choices in a course of study is the degree to which the teacher views the student as an agent of free moral choice, that is as noumenon. The extent that a teacher treats a student as something to be taught and trained is the degree to which the teacher views the student as phenomenon--simply another aspect of the world of space and time, scientifically explainable in a deterministic universe. Thus, the teacher is faced with a dilemma; namely, the degree to which each student is to be treated as either noumenon or phenomenon. Because of the importance of individual freedom within the context of the ideals of the liberal American democracy, the Kantian perspective of noumenon has complex and far-reaching implications for American public education policies and practices.

For example, because science has grown so much broader in its influence on virtually all aspects of society, the problems associated with the application of science clearly are immeasurably greater than it was in Kant's world of the 1700s. This is particularly true in the treatment of human beings as scientifically exhaustible objects. In today's world the degree to which humans can be and in fact are being subjected to scientific treatment is rapidly accelerating and gaining broader acceptance. This is evidenced by the explosion of knowledge and techniques of genetic engineering, the development of *in vitro* fertilization techniques, the use of mood-altering drugs, and the wider application of psychological conditioning processes emanating from behavioristic psychology.[7] Likening the human being to a scientifically exhaustible object, amenable to treatments in the same way as are chemicals and plants, reveals a social value system grounded in materialism. As a consequence of social policies and practices being grounded primarily in a value-free rationality such as science, modern society is beset by moral dilemmas much like those with which Kant had wrestled when he was formulating his philosophical positions.

Implications of Kant's description of reality as noumenon becomes paramount for the modern educator. If Kant was correct and the essential ingredient for all education is indeed "character development" through moral perception of the self, then an educational system which is not based on this premise is inconsistent with the primacy of human existence. To the degree that education becomes essentially scientific, through a grounding in purely positivistic epistemologies such as behaviorism, Kant's phenomenal world, rather than his noumenal world, will instead become modern civilization's view of reality. Thus, if educators ground their practices exclusively in science, then students will be reduced to measurable units, units whose only differences will be essentially quantitative in nature. If carried out over a long period of time this might possibly render the qualitative aspects of human existence meaningless. Consequently, the development of character will have little meaning except at a "scientifically" determined level. In effect, moral freedom will have been lost. If this state of affairs eventually does maintain, then the early Greek atomists' theory, so clearly expressed by Democritus, will once again hold sway; namely, that everything is ultimately reducible to one or more of the same fundamental kind of irreducible particle, *atoma*.

Implications of the Idealistic/Materialistic Dichotomy

Many dilemmas analogous to those stemming from the idealistic/materialistic dichotomy which Kant had proposed in the eighteenth century presently exist in the American society. This is particularly evident in the valuing of knowledge. In this regard it is clear that the intrinsic valuing of knowledge has become less "rational" (acceptable as a reasoned choice) as greater emphasis is placed on the "measurement" of all knowledge. Yet, oddly enough, the valuing of knowledge intrinsically might actually enhance the potential for measuring any and all knowledge. For example, the most effective way of maintaining a healthy body could involve specific rules and guidelines developed from measurable criteria. Such rules and guidelines can become worth doing in and of themselves, that is they might attain the status of being intrinsically valued.

Analogies also can be drawn between the idealistic view of intrinsically valuing knowledge and a materialistic version thereof. For example, it has become necessary, in the materialistic sense, to justify public schools offering specific programs that deal with the proper development and maintenance of the human body (i.e., physical education and health). A myriad of other materialistically grounded programs, courses, or units within courses have been justified educationally solely by their perceived need and/or use. Included among these are "business practices," "safe driving methods," "home care and cooking," "healthy sexual practices," and "appropriate ways of dealing with death," among countless other bits of knowledge that everyone "must" learn.

The competition to have many bits of information and a multitude of immediately useful skills included in the academic structure of public schools is purely political in nature. It is political because the competition is essentially a struggle over which values will be reflected in the curriculum.[8] Value questions in regard to this competition include the following: What counts as the knowledge that children should learn as a part their public school education?; How and when is this body of knowledge to be updated as new knowledge is discovered?; Who among the children is to receive either all or only certain aspects of this knowledge?; Who is to teach such knowledge to the children?; How is this knowledge to be taught?; and, How are the resources to be derived for the teaching of this knowledge?[9] Taking information and skills "useful" only in an immediate sense and incorporating them into the academic structure of public schools comprises precisely this kind of political dilemma. This becomes even more apparent when the inclusion of immediately useful information and skills is justified solely on "scientific" and "technological" grounds.

On the other hand, the idealists' value of knowledge is not predicated on justifying by need and/or use the knowledge which should be included in the academic structure of a school. Rather, they believe that the academic structure of a school should be grounded in the knowledge that reflects the many centuries of human intellectual pursuit as mitigated by human experience. What is more, this fundamental knowledge should act as a framework within which the development of the broadest possible type of knowledge is to take place. Such knowledge would be the most likely to provide the individual with a background for dealing with any and all problematic situations. Thus, since an emphasis on either immediate or distant practical knowledge is essentially instrumental, then it logically can be concluded that idealists must value knowledge intrinsically.

Lest the intrinsic/instrumental model for the valuing of knowledge be relegated to an esoteric level, it must be pointed out that the concept of the intrinsic valuing of knowledge does make a difference in just how a particular society might perceive such knowledge. For instance, the American society views the rights[10] to "life, liberty, and the pursuit of happiness" to be natural rights and not to be compromised in any way by the government. On the other hand, another society might not hold these individual rights to have such a fundamental nature. One example of this might be a society that views the individual as having only those rights given by the state because (1) the individual exists for the state and (2) the state exists for all. In such a society the rights to life, liberty, and the pursuit of happiness would not be of a fundamental and essential value but a value of only ancillary worth at best. It is logical that in such a society choices would have to be made between the personal rights of individuals in contrast to their inherent duties to the state, even though the state has a duty to all individuals.

On the other hand, even though some societies hold the rights to "life, liberty, and the pursuit of happiness" to be fundamental and essential, these individual rights, even in the most liberal of organized societies, must ultimately yield to whatever the state deems important. Indeed, even in the United States, where fundamental individual rights are constitutionally protected, these rights are, nonetheless, reducible to mere legal principles that can be applied by the courts.[11] For example, the government, as the agent for the people, can deny a person life, liberty, and/or the pursuit of happiness as long as the person is afforded the Constitutional protection of substantive and procedural due process of law.

Clearly then, in any organized society--whether the state exists for all individuals collectively, whether the state exists for a particular individual, or whether the state exists for some deity or other ends--individual rights exist only at the will of the government. Consequently, knowledge of an intrinsic worth has a societal reference. But, even if the valuing of knowledge has a societal reference, educational institutions do not necessarily need to have the same reference in order to exist in that society, particularly if the institutions are international in character. For example, universities, at least as they have evolved in Western societies, are not automatically made up of the same kind of knowledge-valuers as the societies which gave rise to them.

It is clear that universities and their professors of knowledge cut across many political and ideological lines. Evidence for this is ample. There are indeed many identical or similar academic disciplines which can be found in the academic structure of nearly all legitimate universities. Despite being separated by significant language differences, professors from different cultures communicate frequently in a variety of forms and on many issues. Examples of this include publications in international journals, joint research and creative works, international societies and meetings, exchanges of faculty and students, and mutual support in political injustices perceived by academicians of one society as being perpetuated upon academics of another society.[12] In addition, the international recognition of knowledge, leading to such acclaimed awards as the Nobel Prize in a number of academic disciplines, suggests a commonality of values which demonstrably surpasses national boundaries.

Individuality and the Intrinsic Valuing of Knowledge

What constitutes the intrinsic valuing of knowledge cannot be negated or neutralized by (1) claiming that scientific and technological knowledge can be valued intrinsically, and/or (2) grounding political and social policies and/or cultural and ethnic beliefs in an ideology--such as logical positivism--that has an instrumental value of knowledge as its base. When societies attempt to do so the outcome is cataclysmic, such as that which occurred in Nazi Germany and Fascist Italy during the 1930s. For any society to be truly free it must not officially promote or sanction any ideology by any means. A government can be prevented from instituting official ideologies only if the rights of individual citizens to believe in any rationality they so desire is fully and unconditionally guaranteed. Once achieved, this state of affairs can only be maintained in a society if the foundation of its system of public education is grounded in an intrinsic valuing of knowledge. This is so because knowledge valued intrinsically is inherently constituted with a potentially infinite rationality; thus, it justifies no particular ideology.[13]

Of all of the institutions in a free society the university, particularly its liberal arts and sciences, has a structure and tradition fundamentally grounded in an intrinsic valuing of knowledge. Through the long and rich history of academic freedom, the foundation of the Western university generally--in a very broad sense--has been insulated from the political machinations of the state. It is this intrinsic valuing of knowledge that must be transmitted to the masses if a society is to remain free. Accordingly, if public education in a free society is to have any semblance of continuity and permanence, then it must have as its primary goal the transmission and protection of this "non-restrictive rationality" view of knowledge. Ideally, then, the essential knowledge of the human race and lessons of history should be discovered, preserved, and taught through institutions that reflect this university ideal to the future teachers of the public schools serving a society.

Little else need be said here about this point except that the education which a society wishes for its young should not be compromised by elements which are either contemptuous of, seek to confuse, or totally ignore the intrinsic pursuit of knowledge. But because of the influence which the university has on public education, a warning about a weakening of the academic structure of the university is nevertheless in order. One of the most insidious challenges to the intrinsic valuing of knowledge in the university, and thus in education generally, is the idea that universities should promote "continuing education." This view, in essence, does nothing more than create the impression within the broader society that the fundamental knowledge represented within the academic structures of universities is merely temporal. Although continuing learning by the individual might be worthwhile, such a "continuing education" should rest on the individual's perception of both what is already known and what more should be known, as it might be grounded in the individual's intrinsically developed knowledge. When, instead, continuing education means "further training," as conceived by someone other than the individual, then the whole meaning of an intrinsically derived and developed university education is negated.

There should be no doubt about the influence of knowledge on the structure of a society. As noted above, the 1930s German and Italian societies are prime examples of how societies can be morally distorted because of false ideologies being reinforced through public education. But false ideologies can also exist as justifications for social structure in societies that lay claim to being liberal democratic in the ideal sense. What must be examined in this regard is the structure of American education and its influence on social structure.

11. Social Structure and Schooling

Historically in America a serious contradiction has existed between equal access to education and the fundamental Constitutional ideals of equality. This contradiction has had devastating effects on the socially disadvantaged. The most notable example has been the denial of quality public education to black Americans. The causes of this particular form of discrimination are deeply rooted in Western culture and, over generations, have been woven into the fabric of the American social order. The venomous nature of racial discrimination in educational opportunities has been manifested in numerous ways. For example, in the pre-Civil War slave states hardships were often imposed on anyone who made an effort to educate slaves. In fact, whites, regardless of social class, who taught even simple reading and writing to slaves were subject to legal sanctions for violating state statutes against such practices. Likewise, they were more often than not ostracized and severely ridiculed by most other Southern whites.

Separate but Equal Policies

By the end of the Civil War the availability of education for black Americans had improved only marginally at best.[14] As the years passed, practically no improvements were made, particularly in the Southern states. In fact, shortly after the infamous 1896 decision of the Supreme Court of the United States in *Plessy v. Ferguson*,[15] in which the Court institutionalized the concept of "separate but equal," discrimination was again legally sanctioned in not only all of the Southern states, but also in many of the boarder and Northern states as well. Although there were separate schools for whites and for blacks, these schools were never equal.[16] It wasn't until 1954 that the Supreme Court, in its historic landmark decision in *Brown v. Board of Education*, declared *de jure* segregation in public schools to be unconstitutional.[17] Nonetheless, the contradictions between the beliefs about and the practices of the democratic ideals of equality are still much in evidence in America. By and large black Americans today experience invidious discrimination and clear economic disadvantages much like those that characterized the legally constituted "separate but equal" social structure of the pre-*Brown* era.

Separate but "Fair" Policies

Although not as clearly evident as racial discrimination, a doctrine similar to that of "separate but equal" exists along social class lines in education. This is a "separate but fair" doctrine that is the basis for the way the system of public education is presently structured. Examples of this include the earlier-mentioned preponderance of vocational schools located in the neighborhoods of students of lower socio-economic status. Likewise, "comprehensive" high schools were ostensibly developed to provide better programs for all types of students. This was to be accomplished by including within the educational structures of these comprehensive high schools not only academic programs for the college-bound but also programs to prepare non-college-bound students for careers in technical or skilled vocations.[18]

The effects of the contradictions that exist between equal access to a quality common education and the American democratic ideals of equality are further intensified by the private and religious schools that claim to be legitimate alternatives to the K-12 public schools. Societal concerns about private and religious schools often center on a tenuous criticism leveled by the advocates of these schools; that is, that there exists a "dual taxation" for the parents who choose to send their children to private or religious schools. This argument is often used to gain political support for a government-funded voucher system for K-12 education.[19] But this myopic view obscures the possibility that a much larger system of private and religious schools, supported by the government through a system of educational vouchers, also might have a deleterious effect on achieving the goal of equal opportunity in American society.

Vocational Education and Social Structure

It has already been pointed out that making "job-outcome" education through vocational programs available in public schools will likely limit the social access of succeeding generations of the lower socioeconomic levels of society. Some of the unfortunate results of this type of educational sifting and winnowing take on the guise of a self-fulfilling prophesy. Social elitists argue that if a society is to function properly, then at least some people will need to work at the menial and less educationally demanding jobs that are necessary to maintain the society. The argument concludes that if this is the case, then society must be predisposed to assure a continual supply of people to perform these menial jobs, regardless of the social inequities which might ensue. On the other hand, paternalists justify vocational education in the belief that more "practical" training for those of the lower socioeconomic levels will better equip them to be "productive" and "successful" citizens after finishing high school.

But arguments for vocational programs in the public schools are fundamentally flawed in that they are not legitimate educational alternatives consistent with American democratic ideals. Institutionalizing within the broad American culture a perceived moral imperative that students in the lower socioeconomic strata need a vocational education in order to be "productive," "successful," and "make contributions to society" seriously undermines the American ideal of equal opportunity. There is overwhelming evidence that educational policies which discriminate in any way prevent succeeding generations of students from transcending social class barriers.[20] Thus, the present structure of American public education, stratified along social class lines, is contrary to the American democratic ideal. The obvious outcome of discriminatory policies and practices in American education has been, and will continue to be, that most public school students from low socioeconomic backgrounds will find it increasingly difficult if not impossible to rise above the social class into which they were born.

Other Criticisms of Vocational Education

Vocational and "career" schooling practices in American education also can be questioned on grounds which are not as obvious as those "educational" practices which have the effect of channeling students into particular jobs. For instance, serious doubts exist as to whether vocational programs can actually meet the goal of preparing students to assume jobs for which they have been trained.[21] Even a cursory analysis reveals numerous programmatic and logistical problems in conducting vocational education programs which make achievement of their goals unrealistic, if not entirely impossible. These problems include the constant need to modify vocational curriculums in order to meet fluctuating "job market" conditions, the necessity to continually re-train faculty, the costly acquisition of modern equipment and the continuous refurbishing of facilities consistent with new curriculum needs, and the continuing demand for a stronger general educational component in the "total" education of vocational school students.

These and many other problems associated with vocational education programs in public schools originate external to and are beyond the control of the schools. The teaching of outmoded skills and the likelihood of continual retraining are among the most evident.[22] Yet the likely reason for the continued teaching of outmoded, non-marketable skills in many vocational schools is not solely due to a lack of information about changes in technical practices in the marketplace. For even if those responsible for vocational schools knew about and wanted to accommodate these changes, they could not possibly alter their curriculums fast enough to maintain the rapid pace of such changes. In fact, it is the political nature of the American public schools to dictate a slowness for all substantive curriculum changes in schools, regardless of their academic or vocational nature.[23] There indeed are many examples of the slow response of vocational schools to meeting changing job market needs. A case in point is that vocational programs which were intended to prepare students to be linotype operators continued to be offered in some schools even though it was clear that the printing industry was adopting radically different technologies.

In addition to changes in job skills being driven by conditions in the marketplace, other external factors prevail which are also beyond the control of vocational schools. These factors would exist regardless of whether the schools were aware of them, wished to do something about them, and for which they could actually change their curriculums. One such factor is that people other than vocational school graduates compete for the same jobs. This is clearly evident in the construction trades where a variety of frustrating dilemmas ultimately confront both the vocational schools and their graduates. Specifically, getting a job in a construction trade for which one has been trained in a vocational school often depends on becoming a member of a trade union before beginning as an apprentice. But, more often than not, one must first actually have a job as an apprentice before being allowed to join a trade union. And, becoming a member of a trade union might be predicated on nothing more than being a relative of a person who is already a member of the particular union. Thus, after being confronted with such a series of dilemmas, vocational school graduates are often less motivated to seek a job which is in any way related to their vocational school training.

It is clear that both internal and external factors give rise to contradictions between the ideal form of education for the American social system and the education received by students in vocational programs in public schools. But, historically, various attempts have been made to restructure the public high school so as to align access to educational alternatives more closely with American democratic ideals.

The Comprehensive High School and Social Structure

The changes over the last one hundred years in the academic structures of colleges and universities, coupled with substantive changes in the American economic system, have prompted significant changes in the academic structure of the American high school. During this era many high schools became characterized as "comprehensive" high schools.[24] Unlike specialized vocational or academic high schools, comprehensive high schools were proposed by educational experts and developed in many communities on the premise that these schools would meet the educational needs of all students, regardless of their aspirations. More importantly, perhaps, was the belief that by requiring all students to take a common core of educational experiences these schools would have the effect of bringing together all social classes. In so doing the uniquely American ideal of equality of education in a democratic society would thus be fulfilled.

But however much the public demands that schools inculcate American democratic ideals, such a policy does not always have that outcome.[25] Public schools are part of a broader society and function through policies formulated by elected school boards. Ideally, these policies should be grounded in a comprehensive educational philosophy that meets the needs of students and society while concurrently being consistent with American democratic ideals. The philosophy thus should be dedicated to providing all children with a comprehensive set of common educational experiences through a "general" education grounded in the moral and ethical foundations of American democracy. But a general education of this nature can only be grounded in the properties of a "liberal" education. Consequently, a contradiction arises in American public education when a truly liberal education is not guaranteed for all children. This contradiction is clearly evident, for example, when comparing the intended outcomes of a common educational core in an idealized comprehensive high school to the in-depth "training" emphasized in a vocational high school.

Idealistically conceived as it might have been, the comprehensive high school and its common core of educational experiences has not lived up to its intended purpose. When considering degrees of comprehensiveness, for instance, the least comprehensive of these schools were located in suburban areas or high-income residential areas of large cities. These "comprehensive" high schools thus were far less likely to have many vocational programs in such occupations as the buildings trades than were schools located in other areas.[26] Consequently, the degree of social stratification of a community clearly dictated the fundamental educational structure of the high school. But even in those comprehensive high schools that do offer a wide variety of both academic and vocational programs the students often have little in common educationally.

Internally, the vocational educational programs of comprehensive high schools are dictated by significant constraints imposed by bureaucracies that administer the various federal legislative acts. Generally, these acts provide large sums of money to local schools in order for them to have vocational programs for their students.[27] Because the regulations emanating from these acts generally require large blocks of the vocational students' school day to be devoted to practical training, little time is left for academic courses. Likewise, because "block" scheduling is used in most high schools, vocational students often attend academic classes with only other vocational students instead of with students from a variety of educational programs. Thus, comprehensive high schools are not often institutions of common educational experiences. Instead, they are institutions of separate educational experiences.

Private Schools and Social Structure

The existence of many private school alternatives has also produced a series of contradictions between the value of an education and American democratic ideals of equality. Among the most glaring of these differences is the development of private academies that have recently multiplied in the South to the extent that they now have become a way of life.[28] These schools were developed to accommodate the large numbers of upper socioeconomic level white children from public schools racially desegregated through judicial mandate. Less obvious are the public schools of the affluent suburbs in the North which, in effect, are fundamentally "private" in nature. They are "private" because those parents who could afford to "buy" a quality education for their children by moving to the more expensive suburbs often did just that, leaving behind the children of the poor who were, most often, black.

In both the South and the North many whites who did initially elect to keep their children in the newly integrated public schools soon sought other educational alternatives, such as also moving into school districts away from the large population centers. Since most non-urban districts were predominantly white to begin with, then having racially integrated schools in either the cities the whites left behind or in the non-urban districts became virtually unachievable. In most instances, the ensuing "white flight" phenomenon led to the erosion of the tax base necessary for the support of most urban public schools. This in turn reduced the money available to provide quality educational programs for the students left behind. Subsequently, the inequities of the original *de jure* "separate but equal" conditions of the pre-*Brown* era were effectively reestablished. But the *de facto* reestablishing of separate systems of education for the poor and the wealthy, and traditional taxpayer resistance to providing quality education in the legally "integrated" schools, nonetheless are social policies clearly contradictory to the American democratic ideals of equality.

To compound the problems faced by American public education, both the expansion of existing and the creation of new non-public school educational alternatives also have created a loose coalition of those opposed to the public financing of schools. These critics of public school finance claim that the tuition and fees incurred by the parents who send their children to private schools is unfair. As noted earlier, the substance of this specious argument is that a democratic society should not be engaged in "double taxation." These advocates of private schools argue that they should not have to pay for both the education of their children and concurrently, through taxes, the education of children in the public schools. This lack of support for financing public education thus has a serious effect upon the public schools in many urban communities, particularly in those having large concentrations of private and religious schools.

Parochial Schools and Social Structure

Many different issues associated with education and social structure in the United States arise when public school alternatives take the form of religious schools. The foundations of these issues are rational myths deeply ingrained in law and tradition. Included among these issues are: (1) the right of the child to be educated in a particular religious environment, (2) the freedom of religion permitting an educational perspective that might be at odds with the prevailing public school philosophy, (3) the preparation and hiring of teachers and administrators dedicated to an education grounded in particular religious beliefs, (4) the utilization of textbooks, library facilities, and other learning resources consistent with specific religious principles, (5) the use of teaching methods which might differ significantly from those of a secular educational system, and, among still others, (6) a desired degree of adequate instruction in religious matters.[29]

These and other fundamental issues separate religious and public schools in the United States and thus impose a severe set of constraints on attempts to achieve the goals implicit in the concept of the "common school."[30] But the clash of democratic theories with the values that underlie educational practices which are inconsistent with these theories is to be expected in systems of public education in progressive democratic societies. After all, few educational value conflicts of any kind are tolerated in totalitarian societies, as these conflicts are resolved or suppressed by their centrally controlled systems of education. The philosophy of education necessary to maintain the ideal American progressive democracy, when compared to that necessary to maintain the model totalitarian state, might in itself constitute the chief ideological differentia of these extreme political systems.

Educational Structure and Political Systems

The *de facto* channeling of students in American education has the same effect that *de jure* educational policies have in totalitarian societies. For example, highly organized totalitarian societies do not permit students to choose a particular form of education. Instead, students are likely to be channeled into a specific educational track, one depending on their natural abilities and how these abilities relate to the needs of the state. Often, "scientifically" grounded testing programs are purportedly the sole bases upon which students are channeled into specific tracks. To what degree such societies might be able to realistically demonstrate that their highly rational system of education actually functions as intended remains questionable. But regardless of the educational effectiveness of tracking systems, the reason totalitarian states have such systems is simply to control the freedom of individual choice in order to meet the purposes of the state. Although the purposes for channelling students into various educational programs in the American society are less clear, they might nevertheless be more pernicious in their effects.

The fact that the theory-to-practice contradictions inherent in American public vocational education receive little publicity suggests the presence of largely uncritically examined educational issues. These issues focus on policies and practices that include: (1) having vocational education programs at the high school level, (2) continuing some vocational programs regardless of their educational shortcomings and their inability to quickly adapt to rapidly changing "market" conditions, (3) the lack of adequate attention given to the liberal education component in vocational programs, and (4) the fact that public vocational school programs disproportionately appeal to the lower socioeconomic levels of society. The blind acceptance of these and other similar educational policies and practices betrays the existence of certain values deeply ingrained in the American culture that allows discrimination to continue to exist in the broader society. The continued sanctioning of discrimination through the perpetuation and maintenance of educational policies will eventually destroy the belief in the ideals of equality, the fundamental ideal of American democracy.

Because education is so important to the achievement of our democratic ideals, then it becomes imperative that public school policies and practices be constantly and critically examined in order to insure that the structure of educational programs foster social access, rather than impede it. Failure to be unremittingly critical of educational policies and practices will instead allow the schools to continue to be an instrument for shaping American youth in a materialism *qua* instrumental valuing of knowledge, the end of which being a rigid social stratification. If the vocational and personal-private views of education continue to grow within the American society, then the gap between a truly free society and a totalitarian state will continue to narrow. In order to reverse this trend toward social control through the solidification of class structures, the contradictions between liberal democratic ideals and the justifications for the educational policies that presently promote social stratification must first be revealed.

12. Distributive Justice and the Educationally Disadvantaged

Historically in the American society, the value of an education has been framed in a philosophical perspective grounded in either idealism or realism. But regardless of the philosophical grounding, Americans have viewed an education as something which a person "acquires" in the process of earning a diploma or degree. Likewise, the "worth" of an educational experience has been viewed to be directly related to the extent to which a person has acquired the necessary cognitive skills to analyze, evaluate, and hypothesize about complex ideas and/or situations. This educational experience, of course, was to be tempered by moral and ethical considerations about the human condition. Because these cognitive skills and attitudes about human relationships were thought to be significantly enhanced through the study of traditional academic fields, then, it was believed, such an education would logically promote a broad philosophical world view and a love--an intrinsic valuing--of knowledge as a whole.[31] But the more modern American view of an education includes an additional dimension to what traditionally had been valued in an education. This dimension is the expectation of some kind of "practical" outcome(s) associated with the process and/or upon completing an educational program; thus, the value of an education now significantly depends on its instrumental worth.

The instrumental valuing of knowledge so dramatically emphasized in twentieth-century America is itself comprised of several utilitarian aspects. The most notable is the growing belief that specific "job" or "professional" skills should be the major outcome of an education. A "job" procurement value is directly related to the development of vocational high schools, technical schools of various types, and certain job-trade-vocational preparatory programs found in junior/community colleges. The "professional" preparation value is directly related to the proliferation of professional schools in institutions of higher education. At the university, for example, professional preparation programs usually range from a four-year baccalaureate degree, such as in engineering, to extended baccalaureate level degrees, such as those in medicine and dentistry. In addition to these general utilitarian aspects there are more pernicious and fundamentally political aspects inherent in a professional education. A particularly significant one is the large amount of cultural capital acquired as a result of being educated to a particular professional level.[32] This value is woven into the structure of American society and disproportionately gives to those with higher levels of professional education significantly more power than others to shape social policy by either *de facto* and/or *de jure* means. Important here for the American society, grounded in the ideal of equal opportunity, is the fact that the level of a person's educational attainment is influenced by many factors beyond the immediate control of the individual.

Financial Support and Educational Attainment

The idea of the public financing a person's elementary and secondary education, at least, has been broadly accepted and is deeply rooted in not only the traditions of American society but in Western societies generally.[33] But there are those who are reluctant to support public education. These include, among others, many who do not want to be financially responsible for educating the children of others.[34] This attitude is to be expected within an increasingly materialistic society. That is, the education of one's own children should take precedence over the education of the children of others.[35]

Consequently, many parents believe that they have personally succeeded chiefly through their own personal efforts and abilities and not because of some abstract "public" performing its civic duty of financing a system of free schools. Thus, the factors these parents have perceived as contributing to their own success they might likewise value in the education of their own children. But such a view of education can also present a problem in that it might have significance only in the eye of the individual beholder.

Inherited and Acquired Factors and Educational Attainment

Certain elements totally beyond the control of the individual, such as inherited genetic factors, play a significant role in the kind of education one receives in American public schools. Likewise, the cultural traits acquired from the immediate social environment in which one is reared is a factor which contributes significantly to later educational attainment. Between the inherited and acquired factors present in the background of an individual lies a continuum of elements which also affects educational achievement. Included among these are a myriad of particular skills and abilities, or at least the potential for acquiring them. These include mathematical, spacial/perceptual, musical, artistic, and linguistic skills and abilities. In addition, the in-herited/acquired factors associated with emotional stability also have a bearing on later educational success. Lastly, the sheer probability of having those physical attributes valued by a given society might play an important role in one's education. The latter include good health, physical size, muscular dexterity, cosmetic features, and among still others, racial and sex character-istics.

It is likely that parents consciously and/or intuitively rely on many factors, including the aforementioned, in choosing the "right" schools for their children. Evidence for this includes the fact that parents often focus their own economic efforts in earning a livelihood on finding the "right" schools. Many will move to different neighborhoods, cities, or even states in order to maximize what they believe to be the best educational opportunities for their children. A relative few even go so far as to move to other countries in order to give their children what they believe to be the "best" educational experi-ences. Nevertheless, the most likely educational alternative available to parents is to move into a neighborhood of the highest socioeconomic level that they can afford so that their children can attend the free public schools located there. When moving is difficult or impossible for many parents, particular for those in the middle or lower socioeconomic levels of society, then parochial schools are a highly valued alternative. A third alternative, particularly for the more affluent parents, are non-parochial private schools. And a fourth option for parents, although one far less frequently utilized, is that of educating their children at home.[36]

Education and Social Class

Clearly, the factors that ultimately determine a person's potential educational attainment are varied and numerous. Many of these factors of course relate to an person's psychological and even physical make-up, but socioeconomic factors inherent in the American society are far more influential in determining educational attainment. Although some parents have many choices available to them in determining the kind of education their children are to receive, there are nevertheless many other parents that have little or no choice in such matters, regardless of the psychological and/or physical make-up of their children. This is due to a variety of socially structured limitations which are beyond the power of the parents to remedy. These limitations, interestingly enough, are the obverse of the genetic\ enviromental factors which the more socially advantaged parents employ for the educational development of their children. For instance, parents with "deficiencies" in their own intellectual, physical, and economic backgrounds are far less capable of making choices for the education of their own children. If the quality of education is largely dominated by the educational attainment of parents, then inequalities in educational opportunity, access, and attainment would likely be passed on to each successive generation.[37] Simply put, those parents who are better educated will likely have children who will be better educated; those parents who are poorly educated will likely have children that will be poorly educated.

It is therefore apparent that the factors which influence educational attainment are contradictory to the fundamental principles of American democracy. The concept of free universal public education might itself actually contribute to a superficial justification of discriminatory educational structures. Many might reason that since every person has a "right" to an education, then they should at least be given educational opportunities commensurate with the social strata within which they exist. For example, those in the middle, upper-middle, and upper socioeconomic levels of society might reason that since children born into the lowest socioeconomic level are required by law to attend school, then it is better to give them whatever education they could best use for practical ends. Likewise, those in the upper socioeconomic levels might reason that they have a right to better schools because they are paying more individual taxes to support public schools than those at the lower socioeconomic levels. Such a Pollyanna view might assuage the consciences of some, but it is hardly a just view. Providing free public schools yet not insuring their quality regardless of location does not fulfill the educational responsibilities of a truly democratic society.[38] If it were so, then the minimal type of education received by the children of the poor would not begin to compensate for the enormous advantages of the children of those in the higher socioeconomic levels. What occurs instead is a perpetuation of the status quo. The children of the poor continue to enter the lowest levels of the work force whereas the children of the upper social strata continue to receive an education that allows them to maintain a higher social and economic status.[39] But, in an attempt to mitigate the effects of the disadvantaged position in which the poor find themselves, society has added a "compensatory" dimension to its ideal of "equal" educational opportunities.

One of the more common examples of a compensatory education for the children in the lower socioeconomic strata is the promise advanced by public vocational/technical education. It is through these schools that the idea of getting an "education" to qualify for skills-oriented and well-paying jobs is constantly publicized. It is likely that the child whose parents are primarily concerned with providing the bare essentials of food, clothing, and shelter will find the promise of a job-oriented education very enticing. Yet, choosing a vocationally oriented education, instead of a liberal education, will literally insure that the child will remain in the lower social strata. Thus, what at first might appear to be practical and "real life" educational opportunities for those in the lowest socioeconomic level is almost surely a social/economic "dead end." It is a future in which there will be many pressures and challenges. These will include demands to acquire new skills in order to meet the needs of ever-changing technologies, continual competition from other unskilled or semi-skilled workers having similar economic and educational backgrounds, continual struggles for wage and salary adjustments, and a realization that no matter how hard they work their children in turn will likely be relegated to the same low socioeconomic level of society. It is a future which clearly few parents in the higher socioeconomic levels would elect for their own children.

The educational attainment of the children born into the middle and higher socioeconomic levels of society are also affected by many factors. Among these factors are parental views of education that are conditioned by their latitude in envisioning, selecting, and fulfilling the educational futures of their children. For example, among those in the middle and higher socio-economic levels there is a wide range of acceptable higher education alternatives which one can select for their children. In the lower levels are those parents who view a junior/community college education as a significant educational attainment. The next level encompasses those who view a local public college as an acceptable institution for their children to attend. In still a higher level would be those who value a state university education. Lastly, at the top of this range of higher education one-upmanship are those parents who would settle for nothing less than their children attending a nationally prominent university, such as one of those in the Ivy League.

The Educationally Advantaged and the Future

The inferences that can be drawn from the present state of affairs in educational selectivity reveals a fundamental contradiction between how the American society fulfills its educational responsibilities and its democratic ideals. Clearly, the complex web of socioeconomic factors that influence educational attainment in America is inconsistent with fundamental American democratic ideals because they perpetuate educational advantages of those who are already advantaged at the expense of those randomly born into the lower socioeconomic strata. Indeed, it is the educationally advantaged that are more likely to receive a superior level of education by not only attending college but by attending the "right" college. Likewise, it is the educationally advantaged that will be able to extend the same, or the promise of even greater educational advantage, to their own children. Also, their increased opportunities to serve as members of local public school boards of education and trustees of colleges and universities will enable the educationally advantaged to more likely perpetuate their own view of what kind of education is "best" for virtually all children. These educationally determined and socio-economic class-conditioned factors place the educationally advantaged into socially strategic positions which enable them to either maintain or break the educational hegemony in America. The path that the present educational elite take, liberation or domination of the masses through the structure of public education, will depend on the fundamental nature of educational experiences acquired through American higher education.

It appears that American institutions of higher education are increasingly adopting the materialistic perspective of education that is so strongly valued in the broader culture. If this be the case, then the graduates of these institutions, who clearly are the educationally advantaged, will likewise pursue a strong materialistic *qua* instrumental educational philosophy as they assume positions of leadership in American education.[40] That these individuals will be largely supplanted by those in the lower socioeconomic strata is highly unlikely. Instead, the educational "leadership" of those in the lower socioeconomic strata will continue to consist largely of simply urging their own children to attend and, at best, finish high school. They are far less likely to be elected or even run for local school boards, make an effort to serve as a college or university trustee, or do anything other than strive to maintain a minimally acceptable level of survival in an increasingly material-istic society.

Unlike the educationally disadvantaged, the educationally advantaged will be able to more effectively utilize their material possessions and social positions in order to engage in activities that are significantly beyond those needed for mere day-to-day survival. Many of these activities are political in nature, thus helping them to obtain positions of educational leadership. In light of this state of affairs there is little hope for breaking the chains of educational hegemony which shackle the less advantaged underclasses. What is needed is a system of free public education that has a structure which is consistent with fundamental humanistic precepts of a liberal democratic society. The grounding of universal free public education in the principles of American democracy might well be the sole means for the American society to eventually extend to all citizens the full benefits of its democratic ideals. To be consistent with these ideals, such a system clearly must have an academic structure that is fundamentally grounded in an idealistic *qua* intrinsic valuing of knowledge. It is precisely such a system of education which can ultimately liberate students from the bonds of their arbitrarily established and politically maintained social classes so as to enable them to freely choose their own futures.

NOTES

1. The courts have been very consistent in interpreting this view of the purpose of public education. As an example, in deciding a case dealing with providing the children of illegal aliens with a free public education, the U.S. Supreme Court said that, ". . . education has a fundamental role in maintaining the fabric of our society. We cannot ignore the significant social costs borne by our Nation when select groups are denied the means to absorb the values

and skills upon which our social order rests . . ." See *Pyler v. Doe*, 457 U.S. 202, 102 S.Ct. 2382 (1982).

2. This perspective on the value of an education for the individual within the context of a free democratic society was clearly articulated by a prominent historian of American education, R. Freeman Butts, when he said that, "...without the proper kind of education, the individual will not be able to develop his own powers as a person. He will not be able to give direction to his own action and thought as he may wish. He will not be able to decide wisely for himself what he should do or think." See R. Freeman Butts, "Search for Freedom: The Story of American Education," *NEA Journal* (March 1960): 332.

3. For a legal view of the relationship of private education to the American society, see *Pierce v. Society of the Sisters of the Holy Names of Jesus and Mary and Pierce v. Hill Military Academy*, 268 U.S. 510, 45 S.Ct. 571, 69 L.Ed. 1070 (1925).

4. For an excellent history of national systems of public education, see Edgar W. Knight, *Twenty Centuries of Education* (New York: Ginn and Company, 1940), pp. 508-82.

5. For a slightly more detailed discussion of Kant's "spiritual idealism," see Hobert W. Burns and Charles J. Brauner (eds.), *Philosophers on Education: Essays and Commentaries* (New York: The Ronald Press, 1962), pp. 81-83.

6. For further discussion of this, see Robert S. Brumbaugh and Nathaniel M. Lawrence, *Philosophies of Education: Six Essays on the Foundations of Western Thought* (Boston: Houghton Mifflin, 1963), pp. 115-16.

7. For a brief discussion of the implication for educational policy of two major and relatively recent advances in science, namely nuclear power and *in vitro* fertilization, see Charles J. Fazzaro, "Some Thoughts on Educational Policymaking After the Events of December 2, 1942, and July 25, 1978," *Proceedings of the Southwestern Philosophy of Education Society* 29 (1979): 156-58.

8. As used here, "politics" is the struggle over the authoritative allocation of values and resources in a society. This is somewhat more formal but not necessarily more accurate than the classic definition by Harold Laswell, "Who gets what, when, and how?" See Harold D. Laswell, *Politics: Who Gets What, When, How* (Cleveland: Meridian Books, 1958).

9. For a more in-depth discussion of the sociological and political nature of these and similar questions, see Richard J. Bates, "Politics, Ideology and Education: The Possibilities of the New Sociology of Education," *International Journal of Political Education* 1 (1977-78): 315-24. For an earlier discussion of fundamental educational questions from a purely academic viewpoint, see Ralph W. Tyler, *Basic Principles of Curriculum and Instruction* (Chicago: University of Chicago Press, 1950).

10. For a comprehensive perspective on rights and education, see Donna Kerr, "Thinking About Education with a Strict Typology of Rights," *Educational Theory* 28, no. 3 (Winter 1978): 165-74. For an excellent general discussion of the rights of children, see Bertram Bandman, "Some Legal, Moral and Intellectual Rights of Children," *Educational Theory* 27, no. 3 (Winter 1977): 170-78.

11. Perhaps the clearest legal interpretation of this notion was made by the United States Supreme Court in its 1943 landmark decision, *West Virginia State Board of Education v. Barnette.* In making it unconstitutional for public schools to require students to participate in the commonly accepted "salute to the Flag" ceremony, the Court said, "The very purpose of the Bill of Rights was to withdraw certain subjects from the vicissitudes of political controversy, to place them beyond the reach of majorities and officials and to establish them as legal principles to be applied by the courts. One's right to life, liberty, and property, to free speech, a free press, freedom of worship and assembly, and other fundamental rights may not be submitted to vote; they depend on the outcome of no election." See *West Virginia State Board of Education v. Barnette*, 319 U.S. 624, 63 S.Ct. 1178, 87 L.Ed. 1628 (1943).

12. There have been many instances of this. Perhaps the most celebrated instance in the 1980s involved Andrei Sakharov, the famous Russian dissident scientist, who was imprisoned because he sharply criticized Soviet military and social policies. Because of his academic credentials many professors in Western universities, at least, openly supported Sakharov and his efforts to gain freedom for himself and his wife.

13. For a more thorough discussion of this idea, see Charles J. Fazzaro, "The U.S. Constitution as a Philosophy of Education: Implications for Rationality and Legitimacy," *Proceedings of the Southwestern Philosophy of Education Society* 37 (1987): 97-104.

14. For example, in 1865, soon after the passing of the Thirteenth Amendment, Congress constituted The Bureau of Refugees, Freedmen, and Abandoned Lands. Known as the Freedmen's Bureau, it had, among its many other responsibilities, the education of the freed slaves. At one point the Bureau supported more than 4,000 small schools that taught little more than reading, writing, and ciphering to the nearly 250,000 who attended them. But

these schools were closed in 1870, thus ending any federal responsibility to improve the education of the newly freed slaves. See Richard Kluger, *Simple Justice* (New York: Alfred A. Knopf, 1976), p. 51.

15. See *Plessy v. Ferguson*, 163 U.S. 537, 16 S.Ct. 1138, 41 L.Ed. 256 (1896).

16. There are many excellent descriptions of the differences between white schools and black schools during the time when separate but equal was the law of the land. One of the most poignant descriptions is that found in Richard Kluger's *Simple Justice*. For example, Kluger noted that, "Separate but equal schools . . . proved a myth from the moment they were approved. In 1910, eleven Southern states spent an average of $9.45 on each white child enrolled in their schools and $2.90 on each black child. And the disparity grew. By 1916, the per-capita outlay for black children dropped a penny to $2.89, but the white per-capita expense rose to $10.32. And the more heavily Negro any given county's population, the larger the gap in the per-pupil outlay." From Kluger, p. 88.

17. See *Brown v. Board of Education of Topeka*, 347 U.S. 483, 74 S.Ct. 686, 98 L.Ed. 873 (1954).

18. Vocational education has been a serious part of American education, at least since the Smith Hughes Act of 1917. This Act provided funds to conduct public high school-based programs designed to develop specific vocational skills. Although heavily funded, vocational programs in public schools have been under constant and unremitting criticisms from many quarters. But the proponents of vocational education have been undaunted in the face of these criticisms. For example, since the early 1970s, the federal government began supporting a program called "Career Education." This is a vocationally oriented program directed at not only high school students, but elementary and junior/middle school students as well. Ostensibly, the purpose of "Career Education" is to encourage students to make wise choices about their future careers. But critics believe that career education is simply vocational education reconstituted. For an excellent example of a critique of both career education and vocational education, see W. Norton Grubb and Marvin Lazerson, "Rally 'Round the Workplace: Continuities and Fallacies in Career Education," *Harvard Educational Review* 45, no. 4 (November 1975): 451-74.

19. Although there have been considerable efforts to gain political support for educational vouchers, little progress has been made thus far. Similar to educational vouchers is the notion of allowing educational expenses to be used as a tax deduction. Likewise, little progress has been made here, except in Minnesota. A 1983 decision of the Supreme Court of the United States established guidelines for citizens of Minnesota in deducting educational

expenses from their state taxes. See *Mueller v. Allen*, 463 U.S. 388, 103 S.Ct. 3062 (1983).

20. For an example of one of the most significant studies of the effects of unequal educational opportunities that shaped school desegregation policy, see James S. Coleman, *Equality of Educational Opportunity* (Washington, D.C.: U. S. Department of Health, Education and Welfare, 1966).

21. Even vocational programs at the community college level, where one would expect students to be more mature in their career goals and their motivation for achieving them, have come under severe criticisms about what they promise students and what they actually provide. For example, many studies have shown that non-graduates of vocational-technical programs have higher incomes than those who are graduates. For an excellent review of the promises and outcomes of vocational education, see Fred L. Picus, "The False Promises of Community Colleges: Class Conflict and Vocational Education," *Harvard Educational Review* 50, no. 3 (August 1980): 332-61.

22. It should be noted that the issue of retraining comes linguistically disguised in many variants. One of these is the modern version of "retraining" which now is referred to as "lifelong learning" and "recurrent education." For an example of the use of these newer versions of retraining in attempts to influence educational policy, see *The Forgotten Half: Non-College-Bound Youth in America* (Washington, D.C.: William T. Grant Foundation Commission on Work, Family and Citizenship, 1988). Also cited in *Phi Delta Kappan* 69, no. 6 (February 1988): 409-14.

23. For an example of studies that have focused on the adoption of educational changes at the school level, see Martin N. Olson, "Classroom Variables that Predict School System Quality," IAR Research Bulletin 2 (November 1970): 1-8, cited in Robert G. Owens and Carl R. Steinhoff, *Administering Change in Schools* (Englewood Cliffs, New Jersey: Prentice-Hall, 1976): 38-39.

24. For a discussion of the American "comprehensive" high schools, see the classic James B. Conant, *The American High School Today* (New York: McGraw-Hill, 1959).

25. Research has shown that the impact which high school civics courses have on middle-class white Americans is minimal. For a discussion of the causes and effects of political socialization, see Frederick M. Wirt and Michael W. Kirst, *Schools in Conflict* (Berkeley, California: McCutchan Publishing Company, 1982), pp. 46-62.

26. See Conant, p. 23.

27. A number of federal acts are important to note here. Perhaps the most significant one was the 1917 Smith-Hughes Act (P.L. 347). This act provided grants for both vocational education programs in public schools and for training vocational education teachers. Other federal legislation that provided more money for vocational education include The Vocational Education Act of 1946 (P.L. 586), the Vocational Education Act of 1963 (P.L. 88-210), and the Vocational Education Amendments of 1968 which increased spending authorization to over $3 billion. For more detail about this, see Stephen J. Knezevich, *Administration of Public Education* (New York: Harper & Row, 1984), p. 225.

28. See Knezevich, p. 263.

29. Many of the arguments surrounding these beliefs have been considered by the United States Supreme Court. The following cases are an excellent resource for these arguments: *Pierce v. Society of the Sisters of the Holy Names of Jesus and Mary and Pierce v. Hill Military Academy*, 268 U.S. 510, 45 S.Ct. 571, 69 L.Ed. 1070 (1925); *West Virginia State Board of Education v. Barnette*, 319 U.S. 624, 63 S.Ct. 1178, 87 L.Ed. 1628 (1943); *Everson v. Board of Education*, 330 U.S. 1, 67 S.Ct. 504 (1947); *School District of Abington Township v. Schempp and Murray v. Curlett*, 374 U.S. 203, 83 S.Ct. 1560 (1963); *Board of Education of Central School District v. Allen*, 392 U.S. 236, 88 S.Ct. 1923 (1968); and *Wisconsin v. Yoder*, 406 U.S. 205, 92 S.Ct. 1526 (1972).

30. The authors certainly make no claim to being the first to realize the importance of a common education to the foundations of a republican form of government. These are Jeffersonian propositions which were clearly articulated in 1848 by Horace Mann in his Twelfth Annual Report when he said that, "Never will wisdom preside in the halls of legislation and its profound utterances be recorded on the pages of the statute book, until the Common School...shall create a more far-reaching intelligence and a purer morality than has ever existed among communities of men." See Lawrence A. Cremin, *The Republic and The School: Horace Mann On the Education of Free Men* (New York: Bureau of Publications, Teachers College, Columbia University, 1957), p. 7.

31. See Henry R. Weinstock, "Philosophical Perspectives as the Antithesis to Education Becoming a Saleable Commodity," *Proceedings of the Southwestern Philosophy of Education Society* 35 (1985): 116-17.

32. There have been many studies to determine the worth of an education. A more recent study on the value of a community college education, as an example, found that, "Community colleges are significantly less able than four-year colleges to facilitate the educational and economic attainment of the approximately 30 to 40 percent of community-college entrants seeking bachelor's degrees. Generally, baccalaureate aspirants entering community

colleges secure significantly fewer bachelor's degrees, fewer years of education, less prestigious jobs, and in the long run, poorer paying jobs than comparable students entering four-year colleges." See Kevin Dougherty, "The Effects of Community Colleges: Aid or Hindrance to Socioeconomic Attainment," *Sociology of Education* 60 (April 1987): 99-100.

33. For a detailed history of the development of state and local tax systems in America, see Jerome R. Hellerstein, *The Development of the American State and Local Tax System*, 3rd ed. (St. Paul, Minnesota: West Publishing Company, 1985), cited in Kern Alexander and M. David Alexander, *American Public School Law*, 2nd ed. (St. Paul, Minnesota: West, 1985): pp. 711-12. For the landmark legal decision justifying the financing of public secondary schools in the United States, see *Stuart v. School District No. 1 of the Village of Kalamazoo*, 30 Mich. 69 (1874).

34. Other groups who at times might be reluctant to support the public schools include those who (1) have no children in the schools, (2) never had children in the schools, (3) send their children to non-public schools, (4) oppose the values being promulgated by the schools, (5) dislike those with whom their children associate in the schools, (6) do not like the background of the teachers, and (7) view the public schools as instruments of political machinations.

35. In this regard, "The view of education as a product, however, can also be readily associated with its being a commodity, much like the purchase of a house, an automobile, a suit of clothes, or the weekly groceries. Since, however, people do not usually give a commodity away, e.g., their house, a car, new clothes, or the week's groceries, then they indeed are unlikely to give an education away. Instead, one rather may save the saleable commodity known as education for one's own children and for one's own self." From Weinstock, p. 119.

36. See John Holt, "Schools and Home Schoolers: A Fruitful Partnership," *Phi Delta Kappan* 64 (February 1983): 391-394.

37. "Given a social order in which there are very wide differences in living standards, in which even minimal living conditions are not satisfied for a substantial percentage of the population, and in which the children of low income families must become wage-earners in their early teens, the mere formal access to primary and secondary education will never provide equality of educational opportunity." See W. T. Blackstone, "Human Rights, Equality, and Education," *Educational Theory* 1, no. 3 (Summer 1969): 288-96. See also, *Brown v. Board of Education*, Supreme Court of the United States, 347 U.S. 483, 74 S.Ct. 686, 98 L.Ed. 873 (1954).

38. For a tightly reasoned argument for disassociating where one happens to live from the quality of education one receives, see *Serrano v. Priest*, 96 Cal.Rptr. 601, 487 P.2nd 1241 (1971).

39. See *Serrano v. Priest*.

40. To this end it can even be said that, "As a consequence, the concept of an education being a **material** product may rapidly be replacing 'the educated person' as being the broad goal of American education . . .. Yet, education in the democratic society which is America is ideally guaranteed to **all** individuals. Hence, an increasingly volatile conflict may be developing between the materialistic desire to keep what one has earned, on the one hand, and fulfilling the idealistic desire to guarantee an equal education to all, on the other." From Weinstock, p. 119.

Five

Social Justice and the Valuing
of Knowledge

Overview

A philosophy of education addresses the fundamental question "What should constitute an eduction?" But in order to be comprehensive and systematic, a philosophy of education must also provide guidance in answering questions about the valuing of knowledge. Such questions must include, among others, "What is to count as knowledge?"; "What knowledge should be acquired?"; "Who among us should acquire it?"; and "How should this knowledge be acquired?" Clearly, these are "ought" or value questions about knowledge; as such they are not questions about what people actually know.[1]

Given its fundamental nature, it is clear that the fulfillment of a philosophy of education cannot be determined by quantitatively measuring selected "outcomes" of educational programs. This is particularly true for systems of public education in democratic societies. Likewise, even at the operational level of schooling, the "success" or "failure" of students on "standardized" tests of academic achievement cannot logically be justified as an exclusive measure of the quality of the academic structure of any educational program in any particular public school. This is a consequence of both the philosophy of education and the academic structures of public schools in democratic societies being considerably more complex than relatively simplistic outcome measurements might imply. Besides this complexity, outcome measures cannot (1) exclusively account for either the fundamental nature of the philosophy or (2) how it was developed. Because these two factors are value laden, they can legitimately be determined in democratic societies only through open political processes, not through processes that are highly rationalized--*qua* "scientific."

Ideally, then, a society that fosters broad public political discourse and action about fundamental social values is likely to have a philosophy of public education which is consistent with its principles of social justice.[2] Consistency between a society's philosophy of public education and its principles of social justice is particularly important for the American democracy because its foundations are grounded in such abstract yet constitutionally guaranteed rights as free speech, individual liberties, and equality of opportunities. For the American society to endure, the abstractness of these guaranteed rights require that they be constantly interpreted within a multi-cultural, dynamic social structure. This can only be accomplished successfully if all citizens are educated to a level that allows each of them to arrive at legitimate interpretations of the meanings of these rights and, through political action, shape their future and the future of all others. Consequently, the philosophy of American public education is a key element in the preservation of our democracy.

A good illustration of the important role that philosophical perspectives of education play in helping citizens fully benefit from the fundamental principles of social justice in America is the continuing controversy that exists between the proponents of Progressive Education and those of an education focusing on the "basics." On the one hand, Progressive educators charge that those advocating "basics" are social elitists because the children from the upper socioeconomic classes are likely to benefit the most from educational programs that emphasize the basic subjects. On the other hand, those demanding a return to "basics" charge that Progressive educators are unfair because the "softness" of Progressive Education denies the children from the lower socioeconomic levels a solid educational foundation.

But this controversy over just *what* the fundamental nature of the academic structures of public education should be is not new. The history of American public education is replete with many "reform" movements which have advocated a wide variety of changes. Many of these movements were highly controversial and fell far short of what their advocates had promised. Regardless of this history of failed promises, the American society continues to tolerate movements to restructure its public schools. The reasons for this are unclear. But in the ideal sense, at least, if the American society was fully aware of the importance of the consistency between a society's philosophy of education and its principles of social justice, then movements to restructure

American public education might well have had a considerably different character.

This is especially true of the 1980s' "reforms" because these reforms are essentially grounded in the epistemology of a social "science" which lays claim to a highly "rational" justification for educational policy, rather than to a justification ensuing from broad political discourse. For example, attempts to use "scientifically" measurable criteria to evaluate the "effectiveness" of many modern educational reforms reveal their proponents to believe that human behaviors can be explained in the same value-free manner as natural phenomena.[3] The objection to this is that it reduces the essence of the human being to that of a mere material object which can be subjected to scientifically grounded, "value-free," treatments.

Like public schools, universities in a democratic society are not immune from inconsistencies arising between their educational structures and the principles upon which they were founded. For example, the expansion of "continuing" education within the academic structures of many universities increasingly reveals inconsistencies between the developing character of the modern American university and its academic heritage. On the one hand, the historic purpose of a university degree has been to equip a student with the cognitive "tools" necessary to become an independent thinker and learner. On the other hand, programs in "continuing" education are justified because they purport to update a student's base of practical knowledge. Likewise, as argued earlier, the academic philosophies and concomitant structures of universities, although not socially as broadly based as public education, nevertheless have direct and fundamental implications for public education.

In order to avoid the shortcomings of both "outcomes-measured" and "continuing" education, it is argued herein that American public education must have as its foundation a theory-based academic structure grounded in a socially legitimate philosophy of education consistent with the principles of American social justice. This is not to say that American public education was ever grounded in such a philosophy. As previously noted, American public education has always been replete with structures which were contradictory to many of the principles of American social justice. These contradictions existed in both the theoretical and practical aspects of education; however, they can be revealed and examined by the use of the intrinsic/instrumental model for valuing knowledge. But care must be taken in the use of this or any appropriate model when examining social constructs which are as value dependent as education. This is particularly important when models are used in combination. For example, confusion and misunderstanding can arise when the intrinsic/instrumental model is superimposed on the philosophic/pragmatic model.[4]

In light of both the theoretical and practical aspects of education, it is argued here that public education in the American democracy must be grounded fundamentally and broadly in philosophical idealism. It is only idealism, with its potential to accommodate an infinite number of rationalities, which can be philosophically consistent with the individual rights inherent in the most fundamental Constitutional guarantee, free speech. It is further argued that the maintenance of this freedom requires that American public education foster two core social values. The first is the principle of "unalienable" individual rights and liberties for each person. The second is the duty and responsibility of each person to unremittingly contribute to the maintenance of these rights and liberties for all others.

13. Traditional Versus Progressive Education: Competing Educational Values

Since at least the 1930s the controversies about the purposes of and practices in American public education have been dominated by policy issues surrounding two competing educational value orientations, namely "basic" and "progressive" education. These different value orientations are reflected in the variety of academic structures present in American public education today, particularly those found in most high schools. As discussed earlier, the development of optional academic structures for high schools created not only many theoretical and factual problems, but, more importantly, problems of equity as well. This happened even though these multiple academic structures were to serve the perceived educational needs of both the individual and the community.

The fact that multiple academic structures exist in the broad system of American public schools can be more easily understood when schools are examined through the framework of the institutional perspective of organizations. This view of organizations is based on the assumption that for an organization to maintain legitimacy it must have structures that are isomorphic with the expectations of the social environment in which it exists. Consequently, in order for a public school to be legitimate it must have academic structures that are isomorphic with the educational values and beliefs (i.e., educational philosophy) of its social environment.[5] In terms of this theoretical perspective of organizations, the existence of a variety of academic structures for high schools in different social settings would thus support the proposition that communities simply have substantially different educational philosophies. But regardless of the role that public schools play in maintaining the pluralistic nature of our society, they must each first and foremost provide a common thread through their educational philosophies. This thread must reflect the principles of social justice held by the broader society as a whole. What is more, these principles can only be propagated through the fulfillment of a philosophy of education which is logically consistent with these principles. This being the case, then a question arises as to whether tolerating significantly *different* kinds of fundamental academic structures for public schools is philosophically consistent with fundamental American democratic ideals.

A School's Philosophy of Education

If, at the theoretical level, the academic structure of a public school should reflect the values and expectations of the community which it serves, then the nature and fulfillment of a school's philosophy of education is the single most important purpose of its educational programs. But it is at the operational level of specific educational programs where problems arise when attempts are made to determine whether or not the educational philosophy has been fulfilled. This is particularly true when attempting to equate quantitative "output" measures of an "educational" program ostensibly designed to fulfill the philosophy.

Since at least the beginning of the twentieth century enormous effort and resources have been used to determine the effectiveness of educational programs. These efforts have been parallel to the "testing" or "measurements" movement in education which began with the introduction of instruments purported to be able to measure a person's Intelligence Quotient (I.Q.). In order to simplify their task, the testing advocates subsequently adopted a rudimentary systems perspective of the schools. This view assumes (1) that knowledge is a transmissible content, (2) that the organizational context within which education takes place is fair, and (3) that education is a social commodity.[6] This unfortunate state of affairs still exists, even though the fulfillment of a school's philosophy of education logically cannot be determined by measuring any specific set of educational program "outputs." This is especially true when these outputs consist of specific bits of knowledge and/or skills that students might have acquired while engaged in the various educational programs provided by the school. The shortcoming of this view is that the problems encountered when attempting to measure the fulfillment of a philosophy of education are problems about values, not problems about facts; thus, these problems do not lend themselves to either scientific or pseudo-scientific solutions or analyses. Precisely because they *are* value problems, their legitimate solutions, at least in democratic societies, exist only as political solutions, and their legitimate analyses can occur only through philosophical analyses.

Given that values constitute a philosophy of education, it is essential for the endurance of a democratic society that its public schools fulfill a legitimate philosophy of education, one logically consistent with the democratic principles of that society. If the purpose of the system of public education in a democratic society is to maintain the society by preparing its citizens to engage in informed moral, ethical, and rational public political discourse, then the philosophy of the system of education must logically be grounded in the principles of social justice upon which the democracy is constituted. If the system of education is structured differently, then the citizens will not be equipped, except perhaps by chance, with (1) the theoretical knowledge to understand the meanings of the democratic principles involved and (2) the practical knowledge necessary to successfully engage in moral, ethical, and rational deliberations about the means of achieving the aims of the principles of social justice upon which the society rests.[7]

Principles of social justice for liberal democratic societies inherently exist at a highly abstract value level. Thus, the education required to understand them, and subsequently to engage in political discourse revelant to the historical context of the society, requires that the wisdom (knowledge) acquired by citizens through the system of public education be primarily philosophical (theoretical) and practical (political). It is philosophical wisdom that provides the conceptual-theoretical maps while it is practical wisdom which allows a person to act in a reasoned and true capacity with regard to the human good.[8] Thus, philosophical wisdom manifests itself primarily through an intrinsic valuing of knowledge best gained in academic structures grounded in philosophical idealism, which itself has no predefined limits or structures. Practical wisdom, on the other hand, manifests itself in moral, ethical, and reasoned actions concerned with things related to conditions of human existence. Since history is in a continual state of unfolding, then the sole measure of the effects of an educational program, based on the quality of both theoretical and practical wisdom acquired by students, must be the endurance of the society itself. But, the endurance of a society is not predicated upon maintaining a static state. On the contrary, endurance might require significant and timely changes in its social structures.

The quality of changes in the structures of a society is a function of the *practical* wisdom of the political actors operating within the political milieu (or *polis*--as in the more comprehensive Aristotelian sense[9]). Subsequently, the quality of the practical wisdom of the political actors is reflected in the nature of their actions or, more precisely, *praxis* ("the disciplines and activities predominant in man's ethical and political life"[10]), which, in turn, changes the base of knowledge from which their actions originated. Viewed in this political context, the actions of the participants must include deliberations about the means for achieving just ends. But the quality of these delibera-tions depends on the quality of the political actors' *theoretical* wisdom; therefore, the determination of precisely what constitutes just ends is not the exclusive province of practical wisdom.

It is in this regard, then, that the philosophy of American public education must first and foremost encompass and address two fundamental aims. First, the schools must prepare citizens to understand the principles upon which the society's system of social justice rest. Secondly, they must prepare citizens to be able to engage in the quality of *praxis* necessary to achieve the principle-based ends of its system of social justice. In the American democracy, the first task requires that students have educational experiences which are theoretical in nature. That is, these experiences must promote the examination, understanding, and creation of rationalities that describe and promote an understanding of our principles of social justice. The second task requires that schools provide real, vicarious, and/or modeled experiences so that students can begin, at least, to acquire the practical wisdom and virtuous character necessary to engage in political activity for the purpose of determining the proper means for achieving a just society.

Clearly then, it is at the operational level of academic structures where schools must provide experiences appropriate for society as a whole to achieve the aims of its educational philosophy and thus the fulfillment of its guiding principles of social justice. And it is precisely at this point where the arguments of the proponents of measurable "outputs" of educational programs lack substance. Knowledge, or in fact anything, that is measurable must first be clearly definable. But the principles of social justice which are the foundation of the American democracy are grounded in abstract values that are in a constant state of definition and redefinition; thus, they are not clearly definable. In light of the social and historical context within which all citizens exist, it is the responsibility of each succeeding generation to understand, interpret, and then take appropriate, just political actions that will lead to the fulfillment of the aims embodied in these democratic principles.

In the United States, the framework and principles of social justice are broadly sketched in the Constitution, particularly in the Bill of Rights. These principles have remained remarkably stable over the 200 years which have passed since their adoption. Interpretation of specific means to bring the full benefits of these rights to all has been left to the political actions of citizens at levels ranging from town meetings to legislative assemblies. The formal clarification of the meaning of these principles of social justice, in light of their historical and social context, has been the province of the Supreme Court of the United States, which itself is made up of citizens. Being a citizens' government, a system of universal public education is essential in order to insure that the system of government itself will prevail. But at the operational level of the public schools many obstacles arise when attempting to fulfill an ideal educational philosophy, particularly if the philosophy is consistent with abstract democratic principles. Although these obstacles often manifest themselves as economic problems, their origins are nevertheless always political in nature.

The Politics of Educational Means

Although the political nature of the public schools provides many means for fulfilling the philosophy of public education, it also establishes many barriers. For example, a society might have as an aim, "equal educational opportunity for all." But it is at the operational level where competition for resources within educational structures is most intense; therefore, the allocation of resources available for providing equal access to educational opportunities becomes problematic, at best. For instance, no particular set of courses or programs exists, regardless of the resources available to any school, that can "logically,"[11] explicitly, and incontrovertibly make the required connections with such abstract beliefs.

What is more, the measurement of a set of "beliefs about education" (an educational philosophy) upon which a school's practices are based is not analogous to giving students specific grades which indicate how much they have learned in a particular course. Nor do student scores on a "standardized" test, such as the *Scholastic Aptitude Test* (SAT), signify the success or failure of a school's philosophy. Similarly, "success" or "failure" of students on any educational criterion does not conclusively prove that a school's curriculum is either a "success" or a "failure." Thus, the structure of the academic programs of a high school, for example, cannot substantiate in the short term, and at best only generally in the long term, that a school's philosophy of education is a reflection of the fundamental cultural beliefs present in its environment.

Likewise, an assessment of the quantity and quality of a school's resources cannot substantiate a school's educational philosophy. These resources would include teaching technologies and organizational policies such as courses of study, textbooks, laboratories, teaching methodologies, counseling procedures, co-curricular activities, scheduling procedures, and parental involvement, among many others. Furthermore, these resources exist solely to enable the teachers to carry out their teaching responsibilities within the broader context of the school's academic structure. It is thus likely that the immediate societal environment upon which teachers depend for their educational resources has a profound influence on their teaching practices. In fact, it is not uncommon for educational resources that come from different environmental levels to cause significant political turmoil at the local district level.[12] These factors become even more important when the role that societal beliefs play in education is critically examined.

The "rational myths" about education held by those who constitute the social environment within which a school exists significantly influence the educational resources of that school. These rational myths, which include beliefs about such things as why taxes should be used to support schools, are part of the fundamental cultural beliefs of the community. Likewise, they also place severe and at times even imperceptible constraints upon the practices of teachers. On a broader scale, a variety of national and/or regional politically influenced and media-publicized changes proposed for education are constantly being debated. This, in turn, often puts overwhelming pressures on local schools to conform to these proposed changes, regardless of their logical consistency with a school's distinctive philosophy of education. In addition, pressures for educational change that originate externally to the system of public education are often triggered by a variety of national and international political events.

The history of American education is rife with examples of changes that followed significant political events within the broader society. One such event was the launching of Sputnik by the Soviet Union in 1957. This dramatic event immediately precipitated severe criticisms of American public schools for what were perceived to be serious shortcomings in their science and mathematics curriculums. Subsequently, and only a short time after Sputnik, efforts to reform high school science and mathematics curriculums rapidly accelerated.[13] But Sputnik was only the triggering mechanism because these reform efforts actually began long before Sputnik. Likewise, these reforms were championed by well-known educators and scientists outside of the mainstream of both the public-education and the partisan political establishments. Prominent among those who wanted to revise the fundamental academic structures of public education were Jerome S. Bruner from Harvard and Jerrold Zacharias from MIT.[14] Many of these reformers were outspoken, like the highly charismatic Admiral Hyman Rickover, who advocated a greater emphasis on technology in school curriculums.[15]

But efforts by reformers to bring about fundamental changes in American public education have been reinforced by many other international political events. Included among these are the Cold War, the nuclear arms race, the "space race," and enormous trade imbalances. These global political events were often accompanied by various political demands grounded in economic and social issues at the national, state, and local levels. The cumulative effect of these external political forces, coupled with the incessant incantations of the many critics within the education establishment itself, created unrelenting pressures on local public schools to make significant changes in their academic structures.

At the national level, these demands for changes in American education pressured the U. S. Congress to appropriate massive amounts of federal aid to finance many of the proposed changes. But attempts to significantly alter the curriculum in the high schools were mitigated by the wide variety of high schools. The policy problems became even more complex when curriculum changes were considered in light of existing differences between similar high schools in different social settings and whether the high schools were parochial, private, vocational, or highly specialized. Thus, both societal pressures for substantive curricular changes and the development of different types of high schools revealed the often contradictory nature and lack of logical consistency between national, state, and local educational policies. This confused state of affairs in educational policy was exacerbated by the lack of a comprehensive, systematic map, a "philosophy," for structuring public education so that it could become logically consistent with American democratic ideals.

The Importance of a Philosophy of Education

It is generally agreed that a logical and consistent educational philosophy can serve as a conceptual map for the fundamental beliefs of a school and how those beliefs relate both to national and state educational values and to the values of the local community. But to be truly functional the philosophy must be a reflection of the wide range of values, from core to operational, held by the community which the school serves. Likewise, the philosophy also must be clearly understood by the community. Although it needs to be flexible, the philosophy cannot be in a continual state of flux or it will become eclectic, reflecting any and all views about the fundamental structures of the school. A philosophy that is a reflection of community beliefs, yet functional and flexible, would instead permit the community to both maintain its educational values and make changes consistent with major shifts in educational beliefs at the broader societal level. Developing such a philosophy requires broad and substantive debate of the issues involved at many levels of society; thus, reaching a consensus from these different levels of society is a very time-consuming, cumbersome process, one often replete with political hazards.

On the other hand, if zealous reformers and politicians did not have to contend with the political structure within which the American society allocates resources and values, then many of the changes they advocate would, if instituted, seriously weaken the very foundation of the American democracy. Fortunately, the Founding Fathers intentionally established many different layers of government in order to prevent this from happening. Their intent, of course, was to insure that government would be continually subject to the will of the people as members of relevant publics, rather than simply serving enthusiastic political elites. Because education plays such an important part in the preservation of fundamental democratic ideals, then a question is raised as to *which* relevant public should be entrusted to make educational policy. Because one of the most immediate and fundamental publics to which individuals belong is their local community, then the fundamental influences and control of the system of public education in the American democracy must logically reside at the local community level. Here, insulated from the direct and immediate control and influence of partisan politicians and massive, unresponsive and complicated bureaucracies,[16] schools and their philosophies can be more easily influenced by the public--the people whose values the schools in a democratic society should ideally reflect.

Consequently, if the philosophy of a school were to be developed entirely beyond the bounds of the community which the school serves, then the school would not truly be a *public* institution. Such a school, removed from the immediate access and scrutiny of the people which it is to serve, would instead become a *government* school--an instrument *of* government rather than an institution for preparing citizens to govern themselves. In the extreme case, a dictator, unencumbered by opposing political forces, could then arbitrarily establish "the" educational philosophy.

Other problems arise when considering the stability of a philosophy of education for public schools in the American society. For instance, if the philosophies are unstable, then the schools cannot effectively contribute to the maintenance of the American democracy. If this indeed is the case, then the point at which the philosophy of any public school needs to have stability becomes paramount. This stability must reflect a consistency that the permanent, fundamental aspects of a school's philosophy maintains with the American democracy; however, this would not preclude that the related objectives or practices might be subject to change. It is thus both theoretically sound and logically practical to refer to a school's philosophy as its "philosophy and objectives," remembering that "objectives" (as used here) means broadly perceived practices or means by which the beliefs about the function of a school are to be fulfilled. On the other hand, these objectives are not to be confused with measurable "outputs," particularly when these outputs are to be used as indicators of a school's effectiveness.

Although this discussion has focused on many of the factors affecting the nature of the educational beliefs and practices of American public high schools, similar arguments can be made for both the elementary and the junior high/middle schools. For example, one of the major, if not the most effective, factors that has had an impact on American elementary schools is the often maligned and condemned Progressive Education movement.

Progressive Education

Today's massive criticisms of American education by its major critics, particularly those heavily involved in the "back to basics" movement, is often grounded in their reactions against the structural changes which have occurred in the schools since the 1930s. These critics hold the Progressive Education movement, largely associated with the great American educator John Dewey, fully responsible for these changes. Yet, Progressive Education in the 1980s has lost the essential ingredients of Dewey's logical philosophy of experimentalism. The effect of Dewey's theory of "knowledge getting" on the education of America's youth initially resulted in modifying the fundamental structure of the curriculum of the elementary schools. These modifications in turn pressured elementary education departments within universities to rapidly change their preparation programs in order to meet the demand for elementary teachers to staff the new "progressive" elementary schools. Since

Progressive Education has a fundamentally different epistemology than that of the arts and sciences, such changes in the elementary education departments soon made them distinct from not only most other academic units within universities but also from other departments within their own schools of education as well.

Likewise, as the elementary schools became increasingly staffed by teachers, principals, and supervisors inculcated with the basic philosophy of Progressive Education, the schools began to develop educational structures which were strongly antithetical to those existing in the high schools. Although the public high schools of the 1930s and 1940s had many differences both among and between them, those differences were neither of the same kind nor magnitude as those evolving in the new elementary schools. In particular, the evolution of "social studies" instead of history, "language arts" instead of English, and "life science" instead of biology, became increasingly suspect by the champions of traditional subject matter at various levels of education. These critics reflected virtually all levels and spheres of American society, be they political, economic, or religious; and, their criticisms where directed at all aspects of what they, at least, perceived to be Progressive Education.

For example, the structure of the progressive curriculum was branded by many critics, particularly the proponents of the "basics," as being anti-intellectual and chaotic. Likewise, the teachers who taught in schools with academic structures grounded in the philosophy of Progressive Education were denounced by the critics as having little or no knowledge of the subjects they were supposed to teach. In turn, the elementary teacher education departments in colleges and universities became the focus of these same critics, who claimed that elementary teachers were being prepared largely in pedagogy rather than subject-matter content. Clearly, it was the lack of subject-matter content that consistently became a major focus of the critics of Progressive Education.

As the number of critics grew and their criticisms became more widely known, a massive "back-to-basics" movement developed. One of the chief protagonists of the movement was the Council for Basic Education, a private organization founded in 1956 for the express purpose of leading America's educational institutions back to traditional subject matter in education.[17] But, by the time the back-to-basics movement developed sufficient momentum to be seriously considered by the general public, the philosophy of Progressive Education, with its radical new approach to the structure of knowledge, was firmly ensconced in most public elementary schools. This institutionalizing of

Progressive Education had been largely accomplished by those teachers and administrators who were prepared in schools of education that had their own educational philosophies shaped by the Progressive Education movement.

This conflict between Progressive Education (child-centered) and the "basics" (subject-matter centered) is still underway within American education. The central focus of the conflict is the philosophical differences between the child-centered educational structure, which dominates in elementary schools, and the subject-matter educational structure, which dominates in high schools. Ironically, the central belief of Progressive Education, that the child is an experiencing individual and that experience must be the central aspect of the child's educational activities, has had little of the effect that John Dewey envisioned. For example, Dewey did not propose replacing the teaching of traditional subject matter with the "whole-child" pedagogy. Nor did Dewey propose such other highly criticized tenets of the Progressive Education movement as the child-developed curriculum, non-directive teaching, and an independent and autonomous "science" of education. In fact, Dewey clearly refuted each of these aspects of Progressive Education which have developed over the years.[18] What did transpire was that the "whole-child" pedagogy which Dewey advocated actually became an end unto itself in the preparation of elementary teachers. In fact, it was only a relatively short time before this narrow emphasis became so firmly institutionalized in teacher-education programs that prospective elementary teachers were almost universally being systematically inculcated with an instrumental view of knowledge, rather than with the traditional intrinsic view.

Aside from the fundamental differences between Dewey's ideal for Progressive Education and the form that ultimately evolved, questions also have been raised about whether Progressive Education is suitable for *all* children, rather than for only those children who have unique educational needs deemed suitable to this form of pedagogy. Justifications advanced for the latter include the special needs of (1) children of lower socioeconomic backgrounds, (2) slow learners regardless of socioeconomic background, and (3) highly talented children who require unique "enrichment" programs. In general, many critics of Progressive Education were not concerned as much about its limited use for special purposes as they were wary about its broad general use.

Progressive Education had achieved its popularity and maximum growth in the 1930s and 1940s. From its inception, it was subjected to constant criticisms from many sources, especially from the previously cited Council for Basic Education. The Council's primary criticism of Progressive

Education was that it ignores traditional subject matter. The Council's philosophy of education is based on several key beliefs. These are in essence that: (1) man is both animal and rational; therefore, his life is not limited simply to adaptation but also involves the fullest degree of spiritual and intellectual attainment; (2) this idea can not be disproved, although it can be challenged by opposing views; (3) therefore, the function of the school is to teach tradition, tradition being the way all past men teach future men; (4) all tradition cannot be taught, then form, order, and hierarchy must be imposed so as to give rise to the "master subjects"; (5) these "master subjects" have "generative powers," among these subjects being those dealing with language; those with form, figures, and numbers; those with the laws of nature; those with man's past; and those about the form and behavior of our planet, the earth; and (6) these "master subjects" cannot be solely sanctioned by need and/or use but are justified by their intrinsic worth.[19] Likewise, the idea of Progressive Education for all children has been challenged by the Council for Basic Education on the same grounds that the Council challenged Progressive Education for children from lower socio-economic levels, those who are slow learners, and those who have special intellectual talents requiring a different kind of education.

Contradictions Emanating From Progressive Education

What the Progressive Education movement has done is to create a fundamental contradiction in American public education. Namely, if a democratic society highly values the basic knowledge inherent in the "master subjects," then selectively requiring only certain students to have access to that knowledge, for whatever reason, is inherently discriminatory. This form of discrimination is evident in the emphasis on teaching job-oriented or work-related skills and "life adjustment" type of courses to economically deprived children.

Skills based on short-range but highly popularized "market" demands have great appeal to those whose home environments are continually clouded by an income barely adequate to maintain a poverty-level existence. All too often, an elementary school education might be the only formal education that many children in the lower socioeconomic strata ultimately attain. Likewise, the fact that the parents of these children are themselves likely to be undereducated merely worsens the problem in that these parents might not make any better-reasoned judgments about the value of an education. Consequently, if the public schools do not provide children with an education that can liberate them from being channeled into specific socioeconomic classes, then the present lack of social mobility will not change and the children of the poor will more likely have a life not much different from that of their parents. In this sense, a job-oriented education becomes an instrument for maintaining a class-ordered society.

Contradictions also hold for children "diagnosed" as being "learning disabled" or "behaviorally disabled." The fact that such children might actually be disabled does not mean that the fundamental tools of learning required to live a full and productive life in a complex society should be different. But acquiring the fundamental tools of learning through education cannot logically be replaced by having a child learn "life adjustment skills," "family living," and the like. Similarly, the perceived need for "enrichment" programs for "gifted and talented" children does not merit a departure from an education that provides the essential, fundamental tools of learning necessary to live in and contribute to a democratic society. In both instances, that of the learning or behaviorally "disabled" child and that of the "gifted and talented" child, the necessity for acquiring the knowledge inherent in the basic subjects is imperative. Because an educated citizenry is a prerequisite to preserving the American democracy, the educational question here is not whether all children should have access to fundamental knowledge. Rather, the question is solely one about what adjustments might be necessary and appropriate in the pedagogical strategies used to teach the subjects, rather than making an adjustment in the basic subjects themselves.

It is because of these and other reasons that the idea of instituting Progressive Education, or some variant of Progressive Education, in American public schools has indeed become the subject of much criticism, especially by proponents of the "master" or "basic" subjects. Although some of these criticisms are justified, many are not. For example, the "core curriculum," an outgrowth of Progressive Education, essentially is based on John Dewey's philosophy of experimentalism; thus, it can legitimately be argued that it diminishes the importance of traditional "master" subjects. But, Dewey did not propose that "experience" should replace subject matter in his pragmatically-based experimentalism. What Dewey did advocate was the need for students to become knowledgeable about scientific subject matter through its practical social applications.[20] In essence, Dewey advocated that subject matter should be viewed as being concurrent or integrated with experience.

Other critics have suggested that Progressive Education was simply a means of dealing with many of the widespread social problems created in large part by the severe economic depression of the 1930s. This view is based on the assumption that: (1) the dire economic conditions of the Great Depression of the 1930s, led to (2) many children roaming the streets, specifically those who could legally drop out of school, hence (3) requiring a massive increase in the appeal that school has for such youngsters, namely making the public school a more desirable place in which to be, thus necessitating (4) a drastic change in the way the school as a whole is to operate.[21] This, in turn, created still another contradiction arising from Progressive Education, namely, the fundamental shift from an intrinsic to an instrumental valuing of knowledge occurring in the public schools.

This shift in the valuing of knowledge in the public schools has been further intensified by more recent attemps to revise public education. These include movements promoting vocational education at the high school level, methods of teaching grounded in behaviorism, the "mainstreaming" of special education students, the inclusion of "adult" and "continuing" education as a function of the local school district, and bilingual education[22] for non-English-speaking students. Many basic education advocates, as well as many other critics of these and similar programs, still exchange charges of discrimination with Progressive educators who promote such programs.

For instance, Progressive educators charge those that advocate a common basic education with being elitists. This allegation is based on the fact that children from middle and upper socioeconomic family environments, because of their exposure to a greater variety of experiences and intellectual stimuli, will far more likely be able to grasp and hence benefit from the basic subjects. The advocates of "basic" education counter the charge of elitism with the argument that if any child does not acquire the basic tools of learning, then the child will be unable to reach the higher, more powerful, and influential levels of society. Viewed in this light, the proponents of "basic" education claim that it is the Progressive educators who, by giving the disadvantaged children a lesser background in the master subjects, are virtually insuring that the already disadvantaged children will remain disadvantaged.

It has further been alleged that many of the fundamental structural changes in public education have diminished the value of the basic subjects, at least in the elementary grades, to the extent that these changes represent little more than educational "faddism." The charge of faddism rests on the argument that the basic subjects invariably have been part of the educational backgrounds of most "successful" people. On the other hand, proposed changes in the curriculum structure which depart significantly from the basic subjects are usually justified as being "useful" (practical) to all students. But this argument can only be supported at the theoretical level; this, the critics

claim, is reason enough to preclude any major departure from an education
traditionally grounded in the basic subjects.

Educational Policies and Principles of American Democracy

This discussion of Progressive Education and basic education illustrates
the necessity for all educational policies that significantly affect the basic
curriculum structure of public education to be grounded in the society's
fundamental principles of social justice. But, the problems of making the
structure of public education consistent with principles of social justice are
very complex, a complexity which is compounded by factors beyond the ability
of the schools to change. For example, regardless of the social system,
children are not born with equal skills and abilities and are reared in a variety
of subcultures; thus, it is difficult, if not impossible, to foster the development
of a congruent set of beliefs that is highly valued by the entire society.
Depending on their nature, the differences in skills, abilities, and value systems
that each student acquires independent and outside of the school can be
viewed as having either positive or negative effects on a child's educational
experiences. But, in such liberal democratic societies as that of the United
States, it is the obligation of society as a whole to make every effort to
neutralize the disadvantages acquired by virtue of birth.[23] Thus, in order to
be an effective instrument in the full realization of the American democratic
ideal, public education must continually seek and implement educational
philosophies complimentary to the fundamental philosophical principles of that
ideal. These philosophies might conceivably be grounded in Progressive
Education, basic education, some combination of the two, or perhaps in a
uniquely different approach or approaches yet to be envisioned.

14. Grounding American Education in
a Democratic Philosophy

Changes in the structure of any system of public education depend
ultimately upon the adoption of a variety of educational policies and their
concomitant practices. For these policies and practices to be legitimate in
liberal democratic societies, they not only must be theoretically explainable
and empirically verifiable, but, more importantly, they must be consistent with
the democratic principles upon which the society rests.[24] This is essential at
both the micro (classroom or school) level and the macro (society) level.
Although policies and practices at both levels should ideally be consistent with

democratic principles, the focus of the following discussion will be limited to the macro level. It is at the macro level where liberal democratic values have a higher level of abstraction and generalization, those having implications for all citizens. Also, as previously noted, the analysis herein is not intended to be prescriptive in every nuance, nor to imply that each phase of the analysis be completely testable and verifiable. Rather, the analysis is presented (1) as an example of what is required of educational policy makers before changes in educational structure are attempted and (2) to clarify the essential differences between "theory-based" and "outcomes-measured" educational structures.

The inferences made about policies and practices in American public education from this analysis essentially rests on two primary assumptions. The first is that there is never a complete consensus within the broad society on the meaning of the fundamental principles of American democracy. The second assumption is that the broader society never fully agrees on the role of public education in the fulfillment of the goals implicit in these democratic principles. These two assumptions, in turn, suggest that because the relationship between educational practices and American democratic principles is at the level of abstract values, then they can never be fully described. *Ipso facto*, this relationships is neither "scientifically" measurable nor predictable. Likewise, because of the complex nature of values in a liberal democratic society, the belief that any measurement of the consistency between beliefs and practices, even at the broadest level, cannot be justified on any legitimate theoretical grounds. The only valid test of the fulfillment of these beliefs is through experience, which in turn manifests itself in the endurance of the society.

Problems of Outcomes-Measured Education

Evaluating educational institutions solely on "measurable outcomes," in the same sense that an automobile assembly plant is evaluated, presents a variety of problems.[25] For the purpose of discussion, consider the hypothetical case of a school that professes to have an educational program designed to prepare medical laboratory technicians. Suppose the course of study in this school is predicated solely on the skills needed to perform current medical laboratory procedures and practices. Being only "practical," the course of study thus precludes the need for incorporating, within the school's academic structures, the medical theory that justifies these practices. True, some fundamental beliefs about the nature of knowledge will likely be part of the basic academic structure, but that belief will totally depend on factors in the medical environment within which the school exists. These factors will be limited to how the broad field of medicine expects medical laboratories to meet its needs at any given time. Thus, the knowledge base of any medical technology school must be derived entirely from the values in the broader medical marketplace. Consequently, if the values held for medical technology are purely "instrumental," then the medical technology school in question will be able to legitimately proclaim that its program of study is entirely "practical." Such a program will likely attract students who highly prize practical, up-to-date applications and skills that can be readily utilized upon graduation. On the other hand, the lack of a theory-based academic structure is what makes a "practical" education superficial, ephemeral, and thus of little enduring educational value for the students.

It can further be assumed that the faculty of this completely "practical" medical technology school would have to possess particular competencies. For example, the faculty will have to be able to: (1) constantly survey the medical marketplace for changes and innovations that have implications for new processes in medical technology, (2) understand the new processes as quickly as they are developed, (3) differentiate between competing processes, (4) extrapolate from the new processes those aspects deemed necessary for training future practitioners, and (5) adapt rapidly to the new processes upon their incorporation into the curriculum. On the other hand, because of the constantly changing academic structure, its students will have to make frequent changes in their course of study in order to be able to at least: (1) adapt their prior training, however immediate, to meet the prerequisites necessary for acquiring any newly defined procedures and practices and (2) after graduation, consider returning to school on a continuing basis, however frequent, in order to remain current with the newest procedures and practices.

If such a medical technology school as described here is to be a profit-making institution, then the ever-changing practical "knowledge" that will necessarily constitute its entire academic structure can be viewed as a positive feature. For instance, the program might be so strongly influenced by rapidly changing innovations in medicine that a "loose-leaf" manual, instead of a textbook, might become the major guide for the course of study. The "loose-leaf" feature of such a manual is significant in that, as soon as new procedures and practices evolve in the medical marketplace, replacement sheets describing them can easily supplant the outmoded sheets. What is more, this will be a relatively inexpensive method for the school to keep the students informed of new procedures and practices throughout their entire academic preparation.

Although this "loose-leaf" approach to "education" might be more efficient, and therefore more profitable for the school, the students will not fare as well. In light of the vast array of ever-changing technological aspects in medicine, what the graduates learn while there will likely be outdated by the time they began their careers. In addition, even if some of the skills that the graduates might acquire remain current, they will will have to compete with graduates from other medical technology schools for the same positions in medical laboratoeies. As a final note, if all goes well and the new graduates are hired, then keeping their jobs will likely require that they engage in some form of "continuing" education in medical technology.

The use of a "loose-leaf" manual for updating an "educational" program points to some of the more "scientifically" desirable aspects of measurable-outcomes educational structures. For example, in the medical technology scenario, measurements could be made of such elements of the structure as: (1) the number of new routines and their related techniques developed over any given period, (2) the amount of time necessary to teach and learn each routine and technique, (3) the performance of each teacher and student, and (4) the cost of new equipment needed to teach these routines and techniques. Yet, these aspects of the program do not describe factors that are educational in nature since they are factors extraneous to the fundamental structures of a truly *educational* program.

The discussion of this "practical" educational program for preparing students to work in the field of medical technology raises a fundamentally important question. That is, "Can any school that claims to *educate*, logically justify on *educational* grounds, an academic structure that consists entirely of easily replaceable subject matter?" It was argued earlier that the worth of any truly educational program can be judged only on the program's ability to provide students with the knowledge needed to make independent, reasoned judgments. Yet, for a democratic society the worth of its system of public education can only be judged in terms of the endurance of that society. But any purely "practical" academic structure is, at best, ephemeral. Consequently, "practical" academic structures for public schools in a democratic society cannot be justified as being truely educational.

Theory and Practice: Competing Educational Values

For any training *qua* "educational" program, a demonstrated need to periodically update the skills of its graduates through "continuing" education might, at first blush, appear to be legitimate. But when the necessity to update skills is coupled with the non-theoretical, end-product, measurable-outcomes "educational" program by which the students had been prepared, then serious shortcomings about the fundamental educational nature of such a program immediately become apparent. Among the most critical of these is the complete lack of intellectual (theoretical) depth within the instructional aspects of its academic structure. This is evident in that graduates of the school wii not be able to adjust independently to the continually changing knowledge required in the workplace. Such a problem is due primarily to the basic premise upon which such a program was initiated; namely, that the program be *entirely* practical. But for any "educational" program to be entirely practical, the instructional dimension of its academic structure must be devoid of a theoretical foundation. The point here is that those who value the immediate use of skills and competencies acquired in an *entirely* practical "educational" program will find it difficult to be independent of their school's "loose-leaf" curriculum. This is due to their "academic" programs lacking theoretical foundations for professional knowledge.

On the other hand, it has already been pointed out that an educational program which in essence is largely theoretical is not likely to have much appeal to those students wanting a job immediately upon graduation. The desire for immediate employment might be so important to prospective students that virtually anything else, including gaining an understanding of the theoretical aspects of their profession, would be at best a minor consideration. Objections to a theory-based educational program might also be raised by those students who simply do not have the ability and/or do not find it intellectually rewarding (i.e., intrinsically valuable) to engage in conceptualizing at a theoretical level.

Lastly, in this discussion of the valuing of theory and practice in educational programs, it should be noted that the concept of "theory," as it is used here, actually means "meta-theory." It is the theory upon which the academic structures of the program itself are grounded; therefore, students in any educational program would not necessarily have to be concerned with the meta-theory of that program. Instead, it is the faculty conducting the instructional dimension of the educational structure who must be totally familiar with its meta-theory. Clearly then, it would be a contradiction for a school to claim to truly educate its students while having a faculty that does not fully comprehend the school's meta-theory--its philosophy of education.

Theory-Based Education Versus
Outcomes-Measured Education

It is unproductive to argue about whether the nature of all educational programs should be either theory-based or outcome-measured. For, after all, the educational ends that prospective students seek *do* play a significant part in determining the nature of any educational program. In fact, an outcome-measured education might well be in order when (1) there is obvious need for people with particular short-term skills, (2) the resources for updating these skills are available, and (3) the students in the program, regardless of their motives, not only seek to learn these skills, but are also fully aware that these skills are short-term. There indeed is a history of such "educational" programs in America. One example is the training programs which the armed forces and other governmental agencies carried out during WWII in order to rapidly train millions of Americans for a wide variety of jobs in the military. In this instance the aforementioned three conditions unquestionably existed for this type of education--the need, resources, and motivation were present. It thus can be surmised that if such an outcome-measured education had not been as massively and successfully initiated, then the American armed forces would not have been able to expand as rapidly as they did. Likewise, the civilian version of military training, broadly instituted, was eminently successful in rapidly transforming a peace-time industrial/business economy into a war-time military economy.

On the other hand, the desire for a more permanent form of education also has been strongly promoted in America. The most obvious example of this is that America historically has supported public education to prepare its citizens to contribute to the betterment of society.[26] In the 1980s, calls for the public schools to emphasize the "basics" and return to the so-called "master subjects" (wherein knowledge is not justified solely by its need or use), are recent, recurring attempts to establish educational permanence in the academic structures of the public schools. But unlike in the past, this form of education, an education with enduring value, cannot be reserved for only a relatively few in the upper socioeconomic strata. It is argued here that if the fundamental principles of the American democracy are to be fully realized for all citizens, then all citizens must have an education of enduring value, regardless of its structure (i.e., basics, master subjects, or whatever).

Theory-Based Education and American Democracy

If the continuation of the American democracy and the fulfillment of its principles of social justice requires that its citizens make informed political decisions, then a theory-based education must be the dominant part of a system of public education. This is particularly true if the American society is to remain democratic in its idealistic assumptions and values.[27] It is highly unlikely that an outcomes-measured education can produce a truly liberal democratic society. What is proposed here is that all members of the American society initially be given an education strongly grounded in theory, equally demonstrable in its empirical aspects, and culminating in the ability to be constructively critical of that society. This logically should have the status of a fundamental Constitutional right to be extended to all.[28] Likewise, an outcomes-measured "education" should be available to those wanting "practical" knowledge, but only after they had been initially educated in the use of theory to guide their social practices. Ideally, then, any outcomes-measured education (i.e., one that is vocational in nature) would take place only after one has reached a level of maturity sufficient to personally make a rational choice about a vocation.[29]

It should be pointed out that the contrasting of a theory-based education with an outcomes-measured education requires further clarification in its own right. For example, a theory-based education is organic-dynamic, whereas an outcomes-measured education is mechanistic-static. That is, they are both educational in the sense that each involves a process that leads to acquiring skills, attitudes, dispositions, values, understandings, or tastes.[30] For a theory-based education, the process is heuristic and the result is dependent upon socially determined contextual contingencies; however, for an outcomes-measured education the process is prescriptive and the outcome is pre-determined.[31]

15. Idealism as the Foundation
for American Education

This critique has revealed serious contradictions between current policies and practices in American public education and the foundations of the American democratic ideal. One of the primary models used here to reveal these contradictions focuses on two valuing domains that are grounded in radically different epistemologies. This model characterizes the valuing of knowledge as being either intrinsic or instrumental. Through the use of this model it has been shown that the contradictions thus revealed manifest themselves in many ways and result in a myriad of both theoretical and practical dilemmas.

Although the complexity of this model is due to many factors, at least two are paramount in making it difficult, if not impossible, to fully comprehend. First, the factors that comprise the fundamental differences between an intrinsic and an instrumental valuing of knowledge have their roots in the cultural contexts of history. Secondly, these factors are of such an abstract nature that they might not be fully definable, particularly where their differences are more subtle. On the other hand, when considering only the discrete qualities implied in its dichotomous nature, this model is ideal for the intended heuristic purposes of this analysis. Likewise, there are models from other knowledge domains, such as those in the humanities, which are entirely appropriate for conducting legitimate analyses of educational issues. For example, in moral philosophy the concepts of social justice are fully appropriate and have revealed significant contradictions in American education.[32] Although the intrinsic\ instrumental model for valuing knowledge has revealed many contradictions between theory and practice in American public education, there have been other models and their concomitant theories that were the primary influence in justifying educational policies and practices. Many of these models and theories have traditionally come from the behavioral sciences, particularly psychology. In fact, it is the knowledge domain of psychology that has been the foundation for many, if not most, of the pedagogical and administrative beliefs and practices in American public schools. This has been especially the case since the early part of the twentieth century.

The justification for using models and theories from a wide variety of knowledge domains resides in the fact that education is basically a valuing enterprise. The problem, then, is not which particular model to use--as long as the model is appropriate in light of the intended purpose. Instead, the problem is essentially epistemological. Because value questions about knowledge are central to virtually every issue in American public education, then these questions must have answers consistent with the principles of the American democratic ideal.[33]

Epistemological Dilemmas in Education

In can be argued that the broad array of concepts, constructs, and theories found in the behavioral sciences, the humanities, or any other legitimate knowledge domain, are historically grounded in one of the two major philosophical perspectives, idealism and realism. Because of their philosophical origins, these two fundamental worldviews can be combined into a purely philosophical framework for viewing education. For purposes here, this will constitute one side of an analytical model. The other side of the model is pragmatism, a framework which is in sharp contrast to one which is purely philosophical. The reason for this is that pragmatism, the more modern worldview, is arguably not essentially philosophical because it lacks a metaphysical foundation. The combining of the purely philosophical and the pragmatic frameworks into a single model (philosophical/pragmatic) is very useful for the analysis of educational issues.

Lastly, superimposing the philosophical/pragmatic model upon the intrinsic/instrumental model provides an even more useful framework for analyzing educational issues. But care must be taken in such a use because this conceptual scheme does not permit an isomorphic relationship to exist between the two basic models. For instance, an intrinsic view of a certain instructional technology (methodology) might not only be accepted but even strongly promoted by pragmatic educators. One example of this would be promoting an educational structure based on the premise that a child can learn best only through experience. Another concept from the intrinsic side of the model, one that is also in the pragmatic vein, would be the "core curriculum" comprised of reconstructed traditional academic subjects. Both of these concepts, the "experiencing individual" and the "core curriculum," are inherent in the educational philosophy of experimentalism advanced through twentieth-century pragmatism in America. These concepts, in one or another form of their many variants, have become so deeply ingrained in American education that attempts at either eliminating or even modifying them have met with an almost unyielding resistance.

On the other hand, the instrumental valuing of knowledge in education also has its antecedents in the philosophical foundations of idealism and realism. For instance, science, which is grounded in philosophical realism, is not completely disregarded by idealists. On the contrary, they consider it worthwhile to learn how scientists think about the universe and how the results of their efforts apply to it. But true idealists never lose sight of how the constructs and concepts of science relate to the essential nature of human beings. Thus, idealists do not consider it important to learn extensive scientific theories, rigorous techniques of observation, and the precise order to follow in reaching conclusions and making inferences. What is of primary importance to idealists is the careful evaluation of the humanistic implications which the outcomes of scientific inquiry might have.[34] This is completely unlike the perspective of pure scientific realism, in which the humanistic value implications of scientific inquiry are essentially irrelevant to the scientific process. Consequently, viewed from the philosophical perspective of the scientist, the idealists' approach to science is one which is in itself largely instrumental.

Idealists also argue that there is little, if any, intrinsic worth in science. Because instrumentalism dominates the foundations of science, there is support for this position. In general, the maxim central to all realism is the principle of *independence*, which maintains that reality, knowledge, and values are independent of the mind.[35] On the other hand, a common unifying factor for idealists is that conceptions of ultimate reality can never go beyond ideas, ideals, spiritual states, or mental capacities. Consequently, idealists reject science as an exclusive means for knowing the "truth," or ultimately reality.

In view of the pervasive influence of science in the American culture, it is little wonder why idealism has not been the dominant paradigm in the academic structures of American public education. Clearly, the intellectual efforts of Plato, Berkeley, Kant, and Hegel--among the many other prominent idealists to enlighten human thought--clearly have not been at the forefront of American public education, particularly in modern twentieth-century America.

In another sense, the high value placed on instrumentalism in the broader Western culture might nevertheless have been the most significant factor in the evolution of the pragmatic movement in the American society generally and American public education in particular. The prominent American pragmatists, Charles Peirce, William James, and John Dewey, found the contradictions between idealism and realism to be irreconcilable. Thus, they largely discarded both idealism and realism as significant means of attesting to not only what is "real" and what is "true," but, more importantly, to what is "good" in human experience. Consequently, pragmatists rejected the central tenets of idealism and realism and put the individual at the center of their doctrine.

The Bridge Between Classical and Modern Education

At the time of Plato and Aristotle the Academy and the Lyceum were primary examples of classical Western education. By the middle of the eighteenth century both Rousseau, the French romantic playwright, and Kant, the German idealist, had been confronted with science, an intellectual movement which, of course, had not faced Plato and Aristotle. On the one hand, Rousseau simply dismissed science out of hand in developing a romantic naturalism regarding the education of children.[36] Central to his view was the belief that society should interfere as little as possible in the growth of the child to adulthood. Kant, on the other hand, did not completely ignore the scientific method on the premise that it is a preconceived basis for describing reality. As pointed out earlier, Kant had instead granted reality to his *noumenal* world, the world of *ding-an-sich*, in which the ultimate causes of sense perceptions are to be found. Thus, for Kant, the primary efforts in education were to be directed toward the development of character *vis-a-vis* the moral nature of the individual. This is a nature that is first and foremost one that the individual not only continually recognizes but also one that must continually be reaffirmed in regard to the individual's possession of free will.

In light of Kant's views of education, it might well be that the essential problem confronting educators is how the child is to be treated.[37] As *phenomenon* the child can be likened to a rat in a psychologist's maze. As *noumenon*, the child is encouraged to understand and accept free moral choosing. Simply put, the more that prescribed subject matter is emphasized in the curriculum, the more the child is likely be treated as phenomenon. The more freedom a child has to choose from a broad curriculum, the more those choices must have both an intellectual and intelligent foundation; but, above all, those choices must be voluntary. It is little wonder, then, that a complex set of problems arise when the curriculums of American high school are viewed from the Kantian perspective of the *phenomenal* and *noumenal* natures of the maturing adolescent.

The controversy surrounding idealism and realism, in regard to which has a more instrumental perspective, and the role of pragmatism versus both idealism and realism, have become more clearly defined in the twentieth century. Darwin's theory of evolution, grounded in scientific realism, had a strong influence on Western society by the latter part of the nineteenth century. Subsequently, the twentieth-century philosophical theories of Alfred North Whitehead and John Dewey, likewise reflecting a variant of realism, came to be viewed as representing appropriate theories to guide "modern" education. For example, Whitehead, resorting to a somewhat mystical interpretation of Aristotle's Classical Realism, evolved such innovative ideas as the concept of three "rhythmic" stages of education. These stages were: (1) the age of romance, up to approximately the age of fourteen; (2) the age of precision, between the ages of fourteen and eighteen; and (3) the age of generalization, from the age of eighteen to around twenty-two.[38] On the other hand, Dewey resorted to the pragmatists' parsimonious way of dealing with what is real, namely through the *experiences* of the individual.

In light of this background in the formation of American educational thought, it can be said that the views of Plato and Aristotle represent the Classical tradition in education, whereas Whitehead and Dewey reflect Modern education. Modern educators subsequently were forced not only to deal with the acceptance of science within the broader society, but they also had to contend with the effects of Darwin's theory of evolution and its variants that linked science to the study and explanation of human behaviors.

Limitations of the Intrinsic/Instrumental Model

A review of the foundations of Western thought and its apparent influence on American education reveals that the inherent issues cannot be fully analyzed by the sole use of the intrinsic/instrumental model for valuing knowledge. Such a bifurcation in the valuing of knowledge contradicts not only the philosophic bases for education, namely idealism and realism, but also any stated pragmatic perspectives about education. Yet, both the intrinsic/instrumental model and the idealism-realism/pragmatism models nevertheless are useful for conducting an analysis of issues in American education. But such an analysis must be undertaken with at least the following two conditions: (1) that the analysis be comprehensive and systematic and (2) that a clear distinction be maintained in the use of these models for subsequently theorizing about education.

Regardless of the models used, it is mandatory that both the aims and purposes of American public education be clearly understood in order to logically formulate any meaningful predictions about the future of the American society. To be legitimate, these aims and purposes must be consistent with the fundamental democratic principles which constitute the foundation of our social order. This analysis has revealed that in order for the American society to endure, public education must be structured from the framework of idealism. This is a consequence of essential nature of idealism. That is, unlike realism or any of its variants, idealism can accommodate an infinite range of the values, which essentially constitute all rationalities. Subsequently, idealism is consistent with the most fundamental of our Constitutional principles--freedom of thought, expression, and religion.

Idealism is also superior to realism as the paradigm for the structures of American public education because idealism has no single concept of human nature or norms by which human existence has to be either explained or determined. Likewise, idealism is superior to pragmatism as a philosophical foundation for public education because pragmatism lacks a theory of reality (a metaphysic) and, thus, is technically *not* a philosophy. Rather, it is is epistemological in nature--a *theory of meaning* with a naturalistic ethic.

In light of both the narrow, value-laden reality presented by scientific realists and the experiential view of the truth advocated by pragmatists, the multiplicity of views of reality held by idealists is of substantially greater worth. Idealism does indeed minimize the use of ungrounded theory and biased-based practices in dealing with the nature of the human being in the ideal form of the American liberal democratic society. What is more, idealism does not depend upon an ultimate view of reality; instead, it relies on certain fundamental enduring beliefs about human nature which have evolved over many centuries.

The physical and biological sciences have demonstrated within their own constituted paradigms[39] certain parameters which scientists claim pertain to all people. But, this does not contradict the preeminence of idealism for educational structures. For example, the quality of food that a person eats is at least as important as its quantity. Appropriate atmospheric conditions, temperature, light, and humidity, among other factors, have been demonstrated to be necessary for humans to be comfortable as well as safe. Furthermore, knowledge about human behavior, in terms of such generally accepted constructs as intelligence, motivation, attitudes, and self-esteem, have been identified as having desirable ranges for maximizing the psychological well-being of the individual.

But, idealism, much like realism, also has been used instrumentally in education in ways other than for simply knowing. For example, idealism has served such purposes as inculcating values of a particular social strata, or the superiority of one race over others. This use of idealism clearly is *not* supported here. The point here is to reaffirm that the factors upon which the structures of American public education should be grounded must be idealistic in nature, so as not to encumber the individual with orthodox views of reality.

Education, the Individual, and the Future

Historically, and particularly in modern American, a variety of "practical" and "scientifically grounded" views of the individual and human behavior have profoundly influenced the structures of society. For example, the scientific management movement of the first quarter of the twentieth century significantly changed the view of the relationship of labor to production. Likewise, these "scientific" views of human behavior significantly influenced the fundamental structures of public education as well.[40] Essentially grounded in realism, these views have ignored philosophical idealism, which initially gave rise to the essence of what it means to be "human." Thus, it is of no surprise that American public education today has a variety of "practical" and "scientifically grounded" educational structures which are based on easily quantifiable and measurable factors. Some of these "practical" and "scientific" approaches to education have at times also aided and abetted the simplistic and narrow "because it works" justification of pragmatism. The influences of these two approaches to education have been so profound that idealism has been either completely eliminated or severely distorted by those in positions to significantly influence American educational policy and practices.

But as realism and its many variants, particularly scientific realism, have gained greater acceptance as legitimate frames of reference for viewing virtually all phenomena, the meaning of the constructs "human" and "individual" gradually have been redefined. The consequences of this has been tragic. The era of Nazism in Germany is but one example of the distortion of the meaning of "human" by those with a view of society essentially based on realism. This distortion also has occurred in Communistic states where it is reflected in an officially sanctioned belief in the "infallibility" of science through the imposition of an almost "non-classical" view of Aristotle's Classical Realism.

What both Nazism and communism have done in more recent times is what many other narrowly bounded social systems previously had attempted. To achieve absolute power through order and uniformity, totalitarian states have invariably attempted to institutionalize--largely through their systems of education--an official government rationality, while systematically purging any idealistically conceived forms of what it means to be "human."

If America is not to be eventually reduced to a totalitarian state, then American public education must have as its total commitment (1) the treatment of the individual student as a unique entity to be (2) educated in a manner that will most likely allow the student to always be guided by a moral disposition to act truly and justly while (3) acting democratically within social groups for both individual and group interests. An education guided by these conditions must of necessity be one which enables the individual to form a symbiotic relationship with the cultural expressions which are unique to the American democracy. To this end, it becomes imperative that at least the structures of elementary and secondary education be grounded in idealism so that competing values can logically exist within the polity.[41] The lack of competing values in a society inevitably leads to the domination of the human spirit.

History has shown that there have always been zealots of realism, aided and abetted by pragmatically justified laws and policies, who would reduce the individual to simply an object to be manipulated, thus disintegrating the true essence of the individual as a human being. At another extreme in the domain of realism, wherein the individual exists solely for the individual, the inherent lack of an ideal to justify contributing to the development of others in the social order would likewise destroy the essence of the human spirit. Either fate is not consistent with the fundamental concepts of the American democratic society. In this regard the individual must contribute to society in a way which will preserve individuality within the context of the larger social group.

Conclusions

This analysis and critique was guided by one fundamental assumption --that the educational policies and practices of a society should be consistent with its sociopolitical philosophy. For America, this means that the structures of public education must be grounded in a world view that is logically consistent with the ideal upon which the American social order was initially founded. This ideal has not only endured but also has flourished, in spite of considerable social and racial strife, a major civil war, two global wars, and several severe economic depressions. History has shown that any one of these sociopolitical factors have destroyed other societies. We believe that a major factor which has contributed to the endurance of the American social/political order is the deeply held value of our "unalienable" rights of free speech, expression, and, above all, thought.

As a consequence of this analysis and critique, we logically make the recommendion that American public education be grounded in a philosophy that recognizes and supports the potential for the existence of infinite rationalities. This is quite different than the pseudo-positivistic realism, often justified on pragmatic grounds, that presently clutters and threatens to dominate the educational landscape. Our conclusions are consistent with the fundamental relationships between the individual and society at large. This is, that American public education must promote the dualistic ideals of both maintaining the essence of the individual and of motivating the individual to reciprocally contribute to society's maintenance of the individuality of all others.

Lastly, this work clearly points to the need for teachers, administrators, school boards, politicians and others who are influential in shaping American public education policy, to engage in *praxis*--informed action--when forces are at work to change the fundamental academic structures of public education. Because public education is under almost continuous pressure to change, they must (1) constantly analyze and critique all educational policies and practices at all levels, from the classroom to the Federal level, then (2) take necessary actions to insure that there is consistency between the means and ends of public education. The framework of the critique that informs the actions of educational policy maker must be grounded in the fundamental democratic ideals upon which the American social order was initially constituted. Only through analysis, critique, and informed action can the public schools be so constituted that they can significantly contribute to the fulfillment of the American democratic ideal.

NOTES

1. For a related discussion about the nature of the fundamental questions that concern educational philosophers, see Hobert W. Burns and Charles J. Brauner, *Philosophy of Education: Essays and Commentaries* (New York: The Ronald Press, 1962), p. 10.

2. The definition of "social justice" used here and in other parts of this book is consistent with that given by John Rawls in that it is ". . . the basic structure of society . . . the way in which the major social institutions distribute fundamental rights and duties and determine the division of advantages from social cooperation." See John Rawls, *A Theory of Justice* (Cambridge, Massachusetts: Harvard University Press, 1971), p. 7.

3. Whether science is value free or not is a topic that has gained considerable popularity with many philosophers and other academics. Those who want to pursue this issue further should start with the classic work of Thomas S. Kuhn, *The Structure of Scientific Revolutions* (Chicago: The University of Chicago Press, 1970).

4. This happens, for example, when an instrumental valuing of knowledge in science (as based on philosophical realism) precludes the scientist from testing an experimental design in light of its humanistic implications (as based on philosophical idealism).

5. For a detailed discussion of this institutional perspective of schools, see John W. Meyer and W. Richard Scott, *Organizational Environments: Ritual and Rationality* (Beverly Hills, California: Sage, 1983).

6. See Wilfred Carr and Stephen Kemmis, *Becoming Critical: Education, Knowledge and Action Research* (Philadelphia: Falmer Press, 1986), p. 24.

7. As used here, "theoretical" and "practical" knowledge are analogous to how Aristotle viewed them in his "theoretical," "productive," and "practical" classifications of knowledge. See Aristotle, *Nicomachean Ethics*, Books V and VI.

8. Aristotle's "practical wisdom" should not be confused with his "productive wisdom." Productive wisdom, or knowledge, has as its aim the making of "things" or products of substance. On the other hand, practical wisdom does not concern itself with making "things" *per se*; it is concerned instead about the conditions of human existence.

9. The definitions of *polis* and *praxis* as used here are intended to be consistent with their use by Fred R. Dallmayr in his book, *Polis and Praxis* (Cambridge, Massachusetts: The MIT Press, 1984, pp. 47-76).

10. Richard J. Bernstein, *Praxis and Action: Contemporary Philosophies of Human Activities* (Philadelphia: University of Pennsylvania Press, 1971, as cited in Fred R. Dallmayr, p. 48.

11. The use of the term "logical" is dependent upon the meaning intended by the user. For example, the idea of the "lay," "formal," and "situational" use of the logical implication in education has been proposed, see Joe R. Burnette,"Some Observations on the Logical Implications of Philosophic Theory for Educational Theory and Practice," *Philosophy of Education 1958: Proceedings of the Fourteenth Annual Meeting of the Philosophy of Education Society* (Edwardsvill, IL: The Philosophy of Education Society, 1958). They have been the subject of extensive discussion over the years. See Howard A. Ozmon and Samuel M. Craver, *Philosophical Foundations of Education*, 3rd ed. (Columbus, Ohio: Merrill Publishing Company, 1986), p. 296-97.

12. One of the most violent examples of this was the mid-1970s' controversy in Kanawha County, West Virginia. The conflict here was over the teaching of the highly controversial curriculum, "Man: A Course of Study" (MACOS). This curriculum "reform" was supported and promoted with

federal funds. Although the violence in this incident was not unprecedented, it was radical for the times. The faction against the teaching of MACOS was so frustrated in its political attempts to change the curriculum that some dynamited the school district's offices. For an excellent account of this controversy, see Franklin Parker, *Battle of the Books: Kanawha County* (Bloomington, Indiana: The Phi Delta Kappa Educational Foundation, 1975).

13. Robert G. Owens and Carl R. Steinhoff, *Administering Change in Schools* (Englewood Cliffs, New Jersey: Prentice-Hall, 1976), p. 40.

14. In September 1959, thirty-five scientists, scholars, and educators met at Woods Hole on Cape Cod to discuss how science education might be improved in elementary and secondary schools. Both Bruner and Zacharias were present. For Bruner's "sense of the meeting," see the now classic book, Jerome S. Bruner, *The Process of Education* (Cambridge, Massachusetts: Harvard University Press, 1960).

15. See Hyman. G. Rickover, *American Education—A National Failure* (New York: E. P. Dutton and Company, 1963).

16. Often, government bureaucracies are considered to be "private governments" in that many of the bureaucrats retain powerful and influential positions for many years without ever having to subject themselves to the vote of the people. In this regard they are undemocratic entities. Consequently, in truly democratic societies, their influence on social policies should be diminished significantly, if not nullified.

17. George L. Newsome, Jr. and Albert J. Kingston, Jr., "A Critique of Criticisms of Education," *Educational Theory* 12, no. 4 (October 1962): 218-26.

18. Robert S. Brumbaugh and Nathaniel M. Lawrence, *Philosophies of Education: Six Essays on the Foundations of Western Thought* (Boston: Houghton Mifflin, 1963), pp. 129-32.

19. See James D. Koerner (ed.), *The Case For Basic Education* (Boston: Little, Brown and Company, 1959), pp. 3-7.

20. In regard to the learning of science, Dewey maintained that, "Adherence to this method is not only the most direct avenue to understanding of science itself but as the pupils grow more mature it is also the surest road to the understanding of the economic and industrial problems of present society." See John Dewey, *Experience & Education* (New York: Collier Books, 1965), p. 80.

21. There is little doubt that the fundamental educational structures of the public schools did in fact change significantly after the introduction of Progressive Education. In discussing these changes, David Swift noted that, "First, punishment is much milder. Second, attention is given to the psychological needs of pupils. Third, many subjects are offered in place of a single academically oriented course of study. Fourth, counseling and testing guide marginal pupils to classes in which chances of failure or frustration are minimized. Fifth, teaching methods take into account the interests of pupils. Sixth, standards of grading and promotion are more flexible. Finally, extracurricular activities appeal to some pupils who would find little else of interest in the schools. In short, every effort is made to make the modern school as pleasant as possible, and these efforts are facilitated by various aspects of what is commonly called progressive education." From David Swift, *Ideology and Change in the Public Schools* (Columbus, Ohio: Merrill Publishing Company, 1971), pp. 31-62.

22. Bilingual education has been advanced by some but condemned by others. Although bilingual education was initially proposed to assist foreign-born students to simply learn English, it was not long after its introduction that other purposes for it were initiated. One such purpose was to enable both foreign-born children and native-born Americans raised in foreign language-speaking households to maintain a strong identification with their ethnic heritage. But a major criticism that has been leveled at this view of bilingual education is that most or all subjects were to be taught in the students' native language rather than in English. As a consequence, these children would most likely have a major linguistic disadvantage either upon entering higher education or the world of work.

23. For one of the more interesting arguments supporting the notion that society has the obligation to affirmatively ameliorate, if not entirely eliminate, social conditions which would be detrimental to a child acquiring a quality education, see *Serrano v. Priest*, 96 Cal.Rptr. 601, 487 P.2d 1241 (1971).

24. The idea of determining the legitimacy of a proposed educational practice by examining it on the basis of whether it is theoretically explainable, empirically verifiable, and socially critical is an adaptation of Jean Anyon's view of just what constitutes an adequate social science. Anyon believes that in order for a social science to be adequate, it must be empirically grounded, theoretically explanatory, and socially critical. See Jean Anyon, "Adequate Social Science, Curriculum Investigations, and Theory," *Theory to Practice* 21 (1982): 34-37. Oakes and Sirotnik apply this more general model directly to change efforts in schools by using a three-part paradigm involving three modes of inquiry. These are: (1) *empirical*, aimed at gathering the "facts" of the situation through objective means; (2) *interpretive* or *hermeneutic*, aimed at probing the meaning or understandings that actors give to events; and (3) *critical*, aimed at exposing and analyzing conditions that lead to the suppres-

sion of the human spirit. See Jean Oakes and K. Sirotnik, "An Immodest Proposal: From Critical Theory to Critical Practice for School Renewal" (Paper presented at the annual meeting of the American Educational Research Association, Montreal Canada, 1983), cited in William Foster, *Paradigms and Promises* (Buffalo, New York: Prometheus Books, 1986), p. 165.

25. For a discussion of the more obvious results of viewing the university as a business, see Charles J. Fazzaro, "The University as a Business, or are Students Like Corvettes," *National Forum* 66 (Spring 1986): 32-34.

26. There is ample historical evidence supporting the desire for an educated citizenry. For example, as early as 1796, George Washington, in his Farewell Address, urged the people to, "Promote, then, as an object of primary importance, institution for the general diffusion of knowledge. In proportion as the structure of a government gives force to public opinion, it is essential that public opinion be enlightened." See Ellwood P. Cubberley, *A Brief History of Education* (Boston: Houghton Mifflin, 1922), p. 288.

27. In regard to America maintaining its democratic idealism, it also seems evident that the "...materialistic nature and instrumental justification of the goals of American education are apt to be producing a citizenry largely incapable of making judgments about educational practices which essentially need to be guided by theory. In fact, there may indeed be few other ways in which a democratic society can simply become just any kind of a society than the lack of philosophical perspective on the part of its people resulting in their reducing education to another saleable commodity . . .." See Henry R. Weinstock, "Philosophical Perspectives as the Antithesis to Education Becoming a Salable Commodity," *Proceedings of the Southwestern Philosophy of Education Society* 35 (1985): 120.

28. Presently, the Supreme Court of the United States does not regard education as one of the fundamental rights guaranteed by the Constitution. See *San Antonio Independent School District v. Rodriguez*, 411 U.S. 1, 93 S.Ct. 1278, rehearing denied 411 U.S. 959, 93 S.Ct. 1919.

29. As the American society is presently structured, making a choice about a vocation generally occurs after completing the twelfth grade.

30. For a thorough discussion of this particular definition of education, see Donna H. Kerr, *Educational Policy: Analysis, Structure, and Justification* (New York: Daniel McKay, 1976).

31. In light of the main purposes of this critique, further clarification of the differences between theory-based and outcomes-measured education are purposively not presented here.

32. The well-known work of Bowles and Gintis would be an example of one such contemporary analysis. See Samuel Bowles and Herbert Gintis, *Schooling in Capitalist America* (New York: Basic Books, 1976). For an excellent example of an abstract theory from the humanities that was used by an economist for the purpose of analyzing social change, see Jacques Attali, *Noise: The Political Economy of Music*, translated by B. Massumi (Minneapolis, Minnesota: University of Minnesota Press, 1985).

33. Richard Bates has stated these knowledge issues most succinctly. They are, "What Counts as knowledge?," "How is what counts as knowledge organized?," "How is what counts as knowledge transmitted?," "How is access to what counts as knowledge determined?," "What are the processes of control?," and "What ideological appeals justify the system?" See Richard J. Bates, "The New Sociology of Education: Directions for Theory and Research," *New Zealand Journal of Educational Studies* 13 (1978): 3-22.

34. In regard to the importance of science as a way of knowing in schools, Louise Antz points out that, "The sciences, for instance, should be taught as conceptual orders having unity and fascinating applications; as open on their frontiers as always in need of new thinkers; as human ideas, partly reflecting nature and partly instrumental dealing with her; as closely related in a two-way process, to other elements in the culture, especially to social life, the arts, morals, politics, religion, and philosophy. *Thinking like a scientist* is something any student can do on some level, and it is far more important than learning masses of facts and carrying out endless laboratory directives." See Louise Antz, "Idealism as a Philosophy of Education," in Hobert W. Burns and Charles J. Brauner, eds., *Philosophy of Education: Essays and Commentaries* (New York: The Ronald Press, 1962), p. 246.

35. See Howard A. Osman and Samuel M. Craver, *Philsosphical Foundations of Education*, 3rd ed. (Columbus, OH: Merril, 1986), p. 32.

36. It is important here to note that Rousseau took a significant shift from the norm of his day in that he viewed the individual and not knowledge as the most important element in the educational equation. His views were elaborated in his famous work, *Emile*, published in 1762. The book was so controversial that it was subsequently condemned by the parliament of Paris, burned, and an order issued that Rousseau be arrested. The theme of *Emile* is grounded in the doctrine of naturalism. To Rousseau education by nature was superior to any other form. Although he believed that children should have the freedom to behave naturally, and thus be allowed to eat, sleep, and play whenever they wanted, they should not be allowed to read books until they are much older. Instead, object lessons should be used to give them social and moral ideas. In short, and as Plato and Comenius had taught, Rousseau believed that children should be allowed to learn about things by

actually doing them. See Edgar W. Knight, *Twenty Centuries of Education* (New York: Ginn, 1940), pp. 350-51.

37. On this topic Brumbaugh and Lawrence state that, "The greater our stress on discipline of the subject matter, the less likely we are to reach adequate respect for freedom; the greater our stress on freedom, the less likely we are to find our students using that freedom with intelligence and experienced anticipation and planning of the consequences of their motives." See Robert S. Brumbaugh and Nathaniel M. Lawrence, *Philosophers on Education: Six Essays on the Foundations of Western Thought* (Boston: Houghton Mifflin, 1963), pp. 115-16.

38. The significant difference between Kant, Whitehead, and Dewey, is that Kant, unlike Whitehead and Dewey, was unaffected by the theory of biological evolution; thus, he did not have to deal with its demands. See Brumbaugh and Lawrence, p. 100.

39. See Kuhn, *The Structure of Scientific Revolutions*.

40. See Raymond E. Callahan, *Education and the Cult of Efficiency* (Chicago: The University of Chicago Press, 1962).

41. For a discussion of the educational implications of values in the American culture, see Henry R. Weinstock and Charles J. Fazzaro, "Educational Implications of Values in the American Culture," *Social Science* 48, no. 2 (Spring 1973): 75-81.

REFERENCES

Alexander, Kern and Alexander, M. David. *American Public School Law*. St. Paul, Minnesota: West, 1985.

Alexander, Kern and Edwin Solomon. *College and University Law*. Charlottesville, VA: Michie, 1972.

Antz, Louise. "Idealism as a Philosophy of Education." In Hobert W. Burns and Charles J. Brauner, eds., *Philosophy of Education: Essays and Commentaries*. New York: The Ronald Press, 1962.

Anyon, Jean. "Adequate Social Science, Curriculum Investigations, and Theory." *Theory to Practice* 21 (1982): 34-37.

Aristotle. *Nicomachean Ethics*. Books V and VI.

Armentraut, W. D. "The Teacher College." In *The American College*. Ed. P. F. Valentine. New York: Philosophical Library, 1949.

Ashby, Eric. "Second Edition/The University Ideal." *The Center Magazine* (January/February 1973): 37-41.

Attali, Jacques. *Noise: The Political Economy of Music*. Translated by B. Massumi. Minneapolis, Minnesota: University of Minnesota Press, 1985.

Baldridge, J. Victor. *Power and Conflict in the University*. New York: John Wiley and Sons, 1971.

Bandman, Bertram. "Some Legal, Moral and Intellectual Rights of Children." *Educational Theory* 27, no. 3 (Winter 1977): 170-78.

Bates, Richard J. "Politics, Ideology and Education: The Possibilities of the New Sociology of Education." *International Journal of Political Education* 1 (1977-78): 315-24.

_____. "The New Sociology of Education: Directions for Theory and Research." *New Zealand Journal of Educational Studies* 13 (1978): 3-22.

Bernstein, Richard J. *Praxis and Action: Contemporary Philosophies of Human Activities*. Philadelphia: University of Pennsylvania Press, 1971.

Blackstone, W. T. "Human Rights, Equality, and Education." *Educational Theory* 1, no. 3 (Summer 1969): 288-96.

Blauch, Lloyd E. "The Pharmaceutical Curriculum." *Higher Education* 9 (October 1953): 26-32.

Blocker, Clyde E., Plummer, Robert H., and Richardson, Richard C., Jr. *The Two-Year College: A Social Synthesis*. Englewood Cliffs, New Jersey: Prentice-Hall, 1965.

Board of Education of Central School District v. Allen, 392 U.S. 236, 88 S.Ct. 1923 (1968).

Bogue, Jesse Parker. *The Community College*. New York: McGraw-Hill, 1950.

Bowen, Howard R. and Schuster, Jack H. *American Professors*. New York: Oxford University Press, 1986.

Bowles, Samuel and Gintis, Herbert. *Schooling in Capitalist America*. New York: Basic Books, 1976.

Boyer, Ernest. *High Schools: A Report on Secondary Education in America*. Princeton, New Jersey: Carnegie Foundation for the Advancement of Teaching, 1983.

Brauner, Charles J. and Burns, Hobert W. *Problems in Philosophy of Education*. Englewood Cliffs, New Jersey: Prentice Hall, 1965.

Breneman, David W. and Nelson, Susan C. *Financing Community Colleges: Economic Perspective*. Washington, D.C.: The Brookings Institute, 1981.

Brown v. Board of Education of Topeka, 347 U.S. 483, 74 S.Ct. 686, 98 L.Ed. 873 (1954).

Brubacher, John S. *A History of the Problems of Education*. New York: McGraw-Hill, 1937.

Brumbaugh, Robert S. and Lawrence, Nathaniel M. *Philosophers on Education: Six Essays on the Foundations of Western Thought*. Boston: Houghton Mifflin, 1963.

Burke, James. *The Day the Universe Changed*. Boston: Little, Brown and Company, 1985.

Burnette, Joe R. "Some Observations on the Logical Implications of Philosophic Theory for Educational Theory and Practice." In *Philosophy of Education, 1958: Proceedings of the Fourteenth Annual Meeting of the Philosophy of Education Society.* Edwardsville, Illinois: The Philosophy of Education Society, 1958.

Burns, Hobert W. and Brauner, Charles J. eds. *Philosophy of Education: Essays and Commentaries.* New York: The Ronald Press, 1962.

Bushnell, David S. *Organizing for Change: New Priorities for Community Colleges.* New York: McGraw-Hill, 1973.

Butts, R. Freeman. "Search for Freedom: The Story of American Education." *NEA Journal* (March 1960): 33-47.

Callahan, Raymond E. *Education and the Cult of Efficiency.* Chicago: The University of Chicago Press, 1962.

Carr, Wilfred and Kemmis, Stephen. *Becoming Critical: Education, Knowledge and Action Research.* Philadelphia: The Falmer Press, 1986.

Case, Charles W. and Matthews, William A. *Colleges of Education: Prospectives on their Future.* Berkeley, California: McCutchan, 1985.

Chambers, M. M. "Diversify the Colleges." *Journal of Higher Education* 31 (1960): 10-13.

Cohen, Arthur M. and Brawer, Florence B. *The American Community College.* San Francisco: Jossey-Bass, 1982.

Coleman, James S. *Equality of Educational Opportunity.* Washington, D.C.: U.S. Department of Health, Education and Welfare, 1966.

Conant, James B. *The American High School Today.* New York: McGraw-Hill, 1959.

Conniff, Richard. "In Chicago: Seminars Everywhere." *Time* (12 October 1987): 12.

Crane, Theodore R., ed. *The College and the Public 1787-1862.* New York: Columbia University Press, 1963.

Cremin, Lawrence A. *The Republic and The School: Horace Mann On the Education of Free Men.* New York: Bureau of Publications, Teachers College, Columbia University, 1957.

Cubberley, Ellwood P. *A Brief History of Education*. Boston: Houghton Mifflin, 1922.

Cubberley, Ellwood P. *Public Education in the United States*. Boston: Houghton Mifflin, 1934.

Dallmayr, Fred R. *Polis and Praxis*. Cambridge, Massachusetts: The MIT Press, 1984.

De Tocqueville, Alexis. *Democracy in America*. Volume II. Ed. P. Bradley. New York: Vintage Books, 1954.

Dewey, John. *Education and Experience*. New York: Collier Books, 1963.

Dougherty, Kevin. "The Effects of Community Colleges: Aid or Hindrance to Socioeconomic Attainment." *Sociology of Education* 60 (April 1987): 86-103.

Educational Research Service. *Summary of Research on Middle Schools*. Arlington, Virginia: Educational Research Service, 1975. 40 pp.

Everson v. Board of Education, 330 U.S. 1, 67 S.Ct. 504 (1947).

Fazzaro, Charles J. "Four Myths of the American University and Their Influences on Its Development." *Social Science* (Summer 1976): 139-48.

_____. "Myth, Metaphor and Educational Policy." *Proceedings of the Southwestern Philosophy of Education Society* 34 (1984): 1-9.

_____. "Some Thoughts on Educational Policymaking After the Events of December 2, 1942, and July 25, 1978." *Proceedings of the Southwestern Philosophy of Education Society* 29 (1979): 156-58.

_____. "The University as a Business, or Are Students Like Corvettes." *National Forum* 66 (Spring 1986): 32-34.

_____. "The U.S. Constitution as a Philosophy of Education: Implications for Rationality and Legitimacy." *Proceedings of the Southwestern Philosophy of Education Society* 37 (1987): 97-104.

Foster, William. *Paradigms and Promises*. Buffalo, New York: Prometheus Books, 1986.

Goddard, David A. "The College of Education Within the University." In *The Role of the College of Education Within the University*. Ed. Anthony Scarangello. Newark, Delaware: University of Delaware, 1969.

Grubb, W. Norton and Lazerson, Marvin. "Rally 'Round the Workplace: Continuities and Fallacies in Career Education." *Harvard Educational Review* 45, no. 4 (November 1975): 451-74.

Habermas, Jurgen. *Toward a Rational Society*. Trans. Jeremy J. Shapiro. Boston: Beacon Press, 1968.

Harper, Charles A. *A Century of Public Teacher Education*. Washington, D.C.: American Association of Teachers Colleges, 1939.

Harris, Norman C. *Technical Education in the Junior College/New Programs for New Jobs*. Washington, D.C.: American Association of Junior Colleges, 1964.

Hartnett, Richard A. "The Pastoral Power of the State and the Autonomy of Higher Education." Paper delivered at the O.I.S.E. Conference on Governments and Higher Education, London, 23 October 1986.

Hellerstein, Jerome R. *The Development of the American State and Local Tax System*. St. Paul, Minnesota: West Publishing Company. Cited in Alexander, Kern and Alexander, M. David. *American Public School Law*. St. Paul, Minnesota: West, 1985.

Hofstadler, Richard and Walter Metzger, *The Development of Academic Freedom in the United States* (New York: Columbia University Press, 1955).

Holt, John. "Schools and Home Schoolers: A Fruitful Partnership." *Phi Delta Kappan* 64 (February 1983): 391-94.

Kerr, Donna H. *Educational Policy: Analysis, Structure, and Justification*. New York: Daniel McKay, 1976.

Kerr, Donna H. "Thinking About Education with a Strict Typology of Rights." *Educational Theory* 28, no. 3 (Winter 1978): 165-74.

Kluger, Richard. *Simple Justice*. New York: Alfred A. Knopf, 1976.

Knezevich, Stephen J. *Administration of Public Education*. New York: Harper & Row, 1984.

Knight, Edgar W. *Twenty Centuries of Education*. Boston: Ginn and Company, 1940.

Koerner, James D. (ed.). *The Case For Basic Education*. Boston: Little, Brown and Company, 1959.

Koos, Leonard V. *The Junior-College Movement*. New York: Ginn and Company, 1925.

Kuhn, Thomas S. *The Structure of Scientific Revolutions*. Chicago: The University of Chicago Press, 1970.

Laswell, Harold D. *Politics: Who Gets What, When, How*. Cleveland: Meridian Books, 1958.

LoPresti, Peter L. "California: The Impact of the Commission on Teacher Preparation and Licensing." *Phi Delta Kappan* (May 1977): 675.

Marsh, Clarence S. "Business Education at the College Level." *American Council on Educational Studies* 3, no. 7 (March 1939): 8.

Martin, Malachi. "The Insignificant Cry of Roger Bacon." *Intellectual Digest* (August 1972): 52-55.

Medsker, Leland L. *The Junior College: Progress and Prospect*. New York: McGraw-Hill, 1960.

Meyer, John W. and Scott, W. Richard. *Organizational Environments: Ritual and Rationality*. Beverly Hills, California: Sage Publications, 1983.

Mueller v. Allen, 463 U.S. 388, 103 S.Ct. 3062 (1983).

Murray, Henry A. "Introduction." *Daedalus* 88 (Spring 1959): 212-13.

National Commission on Excellence in Education. "An Open Letter to the American People, A Nation at Risk: The Imperative for Educational Reform." *Education Week* 27 (April 1983): 14.

Newsome, George L., Jr. "American University Patterns, 1776-1900: A Study of Six Selected Universities." Ph.D. disseration, Yale University, 1956.

Newsome, George L., Jr. and Kingston, Albert J., Jr., "A Critique of Criticisms of Education." *Educational Theory* 12, no. 4 (October 1962): 218-26.

Oakes, Jean and Sirotnik, K. "An Immodest Proposal: From Critical Theory to Critical Practice for School Renewal." Paper delivered at the American Educational Research Association, Montreal Canada, 1983.

O'Connell, Thomas E. *Community Colleges: A President's View*. Urbana, Illinois: University of Illinois Press, 1968.

Olson, Martin N. "Classroom Variables that Predict School System Quality." *IAR Research Bulletin* 2 (November 1970): 1-8.

Owens, Robert G. and Steinhoff, Carl R. *Administering Change in Schools*. Englewood Cliffs, New Jersey: Prentice-Hall, 1976.

Ozman, Howard A. and Craver, Samuel M. *Philosophical Foundations of Education*. 3rd ed. Columbus, Ohio: Merrill, 1986.

Parker, Franklin. *Battle of the Books: Kanawha County*. Bloomington, Indiana: The Phi Delta Kappa Educational Foundation, 1975.

Pierce v. Society of the Sisters of the Holy Names of Jesus and Mary and Pierce v. Hill Military Academy, 268 U.S. 510, 45 S.Ct. 571, 69 L.Ed. 1070 (1925).

Pincus, Fred L. "The False Promises of Community Colleges: Class Conflict and Vocational Education." *Harvard Educational Review* 50, no. 3 (August 1980): 332-61.

Plessy v. Ferguson, 163 U.S. 537, 16 S.Ct. 1138, 41 L.Ed. 256 (1896).

Price, Kingsley. "What is a Philosophy of Education?" *Educational Theory* 6 (April 1956): 86-94.

Pyler v. Doe, 457 U.S. 202, 102 S.Ct. 2382 (1982).

Rafferty, Max. "What Does Your Child Learn in School?." *St. Louis Globe Democrat* (17 November 1969): 14A.

Rawls, John. *A Theory of Justice*. Cambridge, Massachusetts: Harvard University Press, 1971.

Rickover, Hyman. *American Education--A National Failure*. New York: E. P. Dutton and Company, 1963.

Rosenberg, Robert. "American Physics and the Origins of Electrical Engineering." *Physics Today* 36, no. 10 (October 1983): 48-54.

Rudolph, Frederick. *The American College and University*. New York: Alfred A. Knopf, 1968.

San Antonio Independent School District v. Rodriguez, 411 U.S. 1, 93 S.Ct. 1278, rehearing denied 411 U.S. 959, 93 S.Ct. 1919.

School District of Abington Township v. Schempp and Murry v. Curlett, 374 U.S. 203, 83 S.Ct. 1560 (1963).

Serrano v. Priest, 96 Cal.Rptr. 601, 487 P.2nd 1241 (1971).

Sexon, John A. and Harbeson, John W. *The New American College*. New York: Harpers & Brothers, 1946.

Shorer, Mark. *William Blake*. New York: Henry Holt & Company, 1946.

Stern, Joyce D., ed. *The Condition of Education*. Washington, D.C.: U.S. Government Printing Office, 1987.

Stolee, Michael J. *Quality of School of Education Students and Graduates*. Milwaukee: University of Wisconsin-Milwaukee, 1982.

Stuart v. School District No. 1 of the Village of Kalamazoo, 30 Mich. 69 (1874).

Swift, David. *Ideology and Change in the Public Schools*. Columbus, OH: Merrill, 1971.

Sykes, Gary. "Evolution of the Profession." *Forum*. the Holmes Group, No. 1 (1987): 11.

Taylor, Harold. "The University as an Instrument of Change." In *The Role of the College of Education Within the University*. Ed. Anthony Scarangello. Newark, Delaware: College of Education, 1969.

The Forgotten Half: Non-College-Bound Youth in America. Washington, Dy.C.: William T. Grant Foundation Commission on Work, Family and Citizenship, 1988.

"Two Steps Forward. . .?" The Annual Report on the Economic Status of the Profession, 1986-87. *Academe* 73, no. 2 (March-April 1987): 3-17.

Tyler, Ralph W. *Basic Principles of Curriculum and Instruction*. Chicago: University of Chicago Press, 1950.

Weinstock, Henry R. "A Critique of Criticisms of Vocationalism." *The Educational Forum* 32, no. 2 (January 1968): 165-69.

_____. "An Analysis of Issues in Liberal and Professional Undergraduate Education." Ed.D. dissertation, University of Georgia, Athens, 1965.

_____. "Comparing a School of Education to a College of Arts and Sciences and Professional Schools in a University." *Proceedings of the Southwestern Philosophy of Education Society* 33 (1983): 159-64.

_____. "On Philosophical Problems Subject to Ordinary Language Analysis." *Journal of Thought* 6, no. 1 (January 1971): 38-48.

_____. "On Valuing Knowledge Intrinsically in Secondary and Elementary Teacher Education." *Proceedings of the Southwestern Philosophy of Education Society* 34 (1984): 136-40.

_____. "Philosophical Perspectives as the Antithesis to Education Becoming a Saleable Commodity." *Proceedings of the Southwestern Philosophy of Education Society* 35 (1985): 116-20.

_____. "The Concept of *Model* and Educational Research." *Journal of Research in Science Teaching* 4 (1966): 45-51.

Weinstock, Henry R. and Fazzaro, Charles J. "Educational Implications of Values in the American Culture." *Social Science* 48, no. 2 (Spring 1973): 75-81.

West Virginia State Board of Education v. Barnette, 319 U.S. 624, 63 S.Ct. 1178, 87 L.Ed. 1628 (1943).

Wirt, Federick M. and Kirst, Michael W. *Schools in Conflict*. Berkeley, California: McCutchan, 1982.

Wisconsin v. Yoder, 406 U.S. 205, 92 S.Ct. 1526 (1972).

INDEX

MELLEN STUDIES IN EDUCATION